Shoeisms

Working woman's guide to take control
and be the *sassy*, successful woman
you know you can be

Veronica CANNING

NEW YORK

Shoeisms

Working woman's guide to take control and be the sassy, successful woman you know you can be

by Veronica Canning

ISBN 978-1-60037-682-5 (paperback)

Published by:

MORGAN · JAMES
THE ENTREPRENEURIAL PUBLISHER ™
www.morganjamespublishing.com

Morgan James Publishing, LLC
1225 Franklin Ave. Ste 325
Garden City, NY 11530-1693
Toll Free 800-485-4943
www.MorganJamesPublishing.com

In an effort to support local communities, raise awareness and funds, Morgan James Publishing donates one percent of all book sales for the life of each book to Habitat for Humanity. Get involved today, visit **www.HelpHabitatForHumanity.org.**

This book is dedicated to my husband, Peter,
my children Amber and Christopher
who make my life a joy.

Contents

III Fall:

conserving space; adopt strategies to conserve your essence

IV Winter:

regenerating space; take stock, refocus on the positives, prioritize

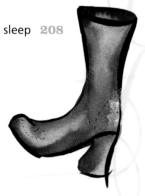

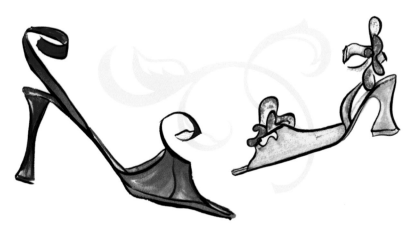

Introduction

I love shoes and have always loved them. I fell for the Cinderella line a long time ago – not the prince, just the shoe. I now realize that I am not alone, because shoes have a special place in most women's lives.

Shoes are magical and have many meanings for me, so you won't be surprised that, when writing this book for women, I knew it had to involve shoes. From there, it was a very small step to inventing the term 'Shoeisms' to encapsulate the elusive magic of shoes within my work.

Starting with creative, fanciful and stylish shoe images, I aimed to write for thoughtful, enquiring, stylish women who choose to query everything in their lives and to look at the world from atop their magical shoes.

This book is not for the woman who likes an uneventful life – it is for a woman who is wrestling with the world, working on herself to be the most wonderful woman she can possibly be.

We know that change is our new reality. Nothing is the same today as yesterday and it will be completely different tomorrow. Finding your place in the world as an accomplished, powerful woman just got more difficult – way more difficult.

Pass on if you think that this is a self-help bible. It is not. To survive, you need more than a list of dos and don'ts – you'll need to know and understand yourself a lot better. You need to examine your every thought and not get stuck in your own way. This book will get you to think for yourself and to find your own powerful place on your own terms.

⤳ Shoeisms are thought changers ⤳

The value of fresh thoughts cannot be overstated. They are the seeds for all of our lives. Never before have we needed new thinking and inspiration as much as we do now – we are on completely new ground and little of the previous thinking can help us now. The scale and complexity of our problems means that we have to radically change our analysis, our thinking and our solutions.

The established way of looking at things has gone, and everything is different now. It is a world filled with endless opportunities for fresh thoughts and ideas, and to capitalize on this newness, we need to change our perceptions and thought patterns. The way is open for complete reinvention if we just rise to the challenge.

One way of thinking led us to where we are now. It goes without saying that we must now have different thinking to lead us on. You must have courage and develop your own thoughts.

⤳ Shoeisms are thought provokers ⤳

They will get you to look differently at your life.

While we wait for the politicians and economists to find new answers, we must get on with our own lives. You have a free choice how to respond; you can ignore the change and act the same way, as denial has a certain seduction – but not for long.

Every day is giving us a new challenge and this can affect your thinking in many, many ways.

The Shoeisms represent a huge opportunity for you. They will challenge your assumptions and will work you through to a clearer understanding of yourself and your place in the world.

They will act as a powerful guide, helping you to become clearer in your thinking, your core values and your priorities.

✒ Shoeisms are a practical toolkit ✒

They form an irresistible toolkit for being a powerful, thoughtful, optimistic and energizing woman and they will take you there in easy steps. I have been a working mother for 25 years and I've learnt the hard way how precious time and effort is for business women so I have made the Shoeisms totally practical and all the advice can be acted on instantly.

The Shoeisms book is laid out in four seasons - each representing a different time in a woman's life. Our thinking changes as we go through these different phases: spring is a time of regeneration, summer a time to thrive, fall a time to conserve energy and winter a time to renew.

Please use the Shoeisms book in whatever way you need to find your own unique way. The book is laid out so that you can read right through it, or just dip into Shoeisms as you need.

I wish you well in your quest to become the best that you can possibly be and I would love to hear from you. Let me know how you are winning.

Veronica Canning

Veronica Canning
info@veronicacanning.com

Spring

As I sat down to write the spring Shoeisms, I was thinking of how my family approached spring when I was growing up and how it has influenced my approach to life.

We operated on the belief, as did a lot of families in Ireland, that if you don't get on top of your garden by St Patrick's Day, March 17th, it will get on top of you. Consequently, there was an urgency to clear out the old to allow creativity to enter.

I have carried this view of getting ahead of the weeds into adult life. Each spring, I have an urge to clear out all the accumulations of the winter and start afresh. I love having creative planning sessions and scoping out the whole year ahead. I also believe in a total refreshing of my business, as I know you need to drop about twenty per cent of your activities each year to stay vibrant and relevant.

So I wrote the spring Shoeisms with this viewpoint in mind. I believe that each of us has a responsibility to ourselves to spend time in a creative space, regenerating ourselves and our thoughts. We not only deserve but also need to have dreams to guide us through life.

John O'Donohue, in his beautiful book Exploring Our Hunger To Belong speaks about life being a pilgrimage of discovery.

"Ideally, a human life should be a constant pilgrimage of discovery. The most exciting discoveries happen at the frontiers. When you come to know something, you come closer to yourself and the world. .... Nature comes to know itself anew in your discoveries. Creative human thought adds to the brightness of the world."

These spring Shoeisms are designed to have your thoughts add to the brightness of your world. They are to help you to lift your spirits, encourage your creativity, and remove the barriers to new thinking – and to get you out of your own way.

There are 14 thought-provoking spring Shoeisms designed to regenerate your thinking patterns and to shift you to thinking about new ideas, taking baby steps at first, to help you develop many more positive thoughts. Go on, clean out the garden, get ahead of the weeds.

Keep an idea box

We all have ideas flashing in and out of our minds but rarely do we systematically collect them. I want you to begin to trust your own thoughts and to collect and value them.

Each action affects your Big Audacious Aim

You can't believe the profound effect of realizing that every action has a consequence. In this uncertain time, snatch some certainty for yourself.

Take baby steps

We all need to encourage ourselves, and taking the pragmatic view that every dream begins with the first step and progresses in subsequent baby steps is an energizing thought.

Everything you ever wanted is on the other side of fear

In spring, you plant things and nourish them; you want to embrace the hope of new things. Fear is the enemy of hope, and as we all have fear, the challenge is to think about the state beyond fear, to see it as a real place and to make it a destination for you.

Believe in yourself

There is no greater thought changer than this one. You absolutely must believe in yourself to cope with the present situation. It is not possible to create new opportunities for yourself and break out of old habits if you do not have a bedrock of self-belief.

Abandon the twin fears

Amazingly, we are equally afraid of success as failure. If you thought fear of failure was the big one, then use this Shoeism to unveil its twin sister. It is vital to know about your fears, to embrace them. So in the Spring phase of encouraging new thoughts, be shrewd enough to know the power of fear and let the air in to dispel the impact.

Change your thoughts

The world is changing every hour of every day at a rate never seen before. The internet has speeded things up to such an extent that information can go global in seconds. Keep up. You must change your thoughts at the speed of the change in your life, otherwise you will get left behind.

Know your hot spots and control them

When you are in the generative frame of mind – thinking new thoughts and seeing only possibilities – you need to guard against your old Pavlovian responses to events. We all have hotspots which can trigger predictable reactions when touched. Learn about them so that you can control them.

Even when you fall, you fall forward

Be a risk taker. Innovation needs courage, so use this Shoeism to give yourself a dose of courage. Change your thinking and believe that the risk of doing something new is worth it by telling yourself that every fall really does bring you forward to a new place.

End each week by making your plan for the next week

Up your chances of success by indulging in a little disciplined thinking and planning. This one little gem is a powerful tool. Take a view of your week on Friday and learn from what has happened.

Until now

We all need simple tools in our toolkit that we can take out and use to get an immediate effect. This Shoeism introduces you to the two magic phrases designed to give you an instant mood shifter. Study them and incorporate them into your everyday thinking.

Act like a tortoise

Meet Aesop's characters, the tortoise and the hare, and learn the simplicity of old wisdom. As you strive to remain positive and generate new ideas and new solutions to your problems, you need to know the difference between panicky reactionary behavior and more thoughtful actions. Examine this and introduce a deceptively simple Shoeism into your life.

Write morning pages

This is one of the most powerful ways of accessing your creativity. All it takes is pen and paper, time and discipline. I guarantee you that the rewards are well worth the effort. Look at this Shoeism if you are having trouble getting your creative spirit working – it is so simple, yet so powerful.

You would be great if you got out of your own way

This is the last Shoeism in the spring section – but really the most liberating one. I firmly believe that the biggest obstacle we face everyday is ourselves. We guilt ourselves, we frighten ourselves, we doubt ourselves. Imagine the transformation if you simply decided to step cleanly out of your own way.

Unleash the fever of Spring and see what new thoughts you have

"It's spring fever. That is what the name of it is. And when you've got it, you want – oh, you don't quite know what it is you do want, but it just fairly makes your heart ache, you want it so!" Mark Twain

Keep an idea box

Get a box of 4x8 cards and keep it in your bag or briefcase. You could also use a small notebook.

Every time you get an idea, capture it. Write it down. It doesn't matter if you don't read it for a while.

You know all your ideas are safe. You will be amazed at how fruitful this exercise is.

⤳ The idea box ⟿

Buy some small note cards and use them to capture ideas as they occur to you. Keep the idea box on your desk and keep adding to it the cards with the ideas. Constantly empty your handbag, your briefcase, your pockets and your conference folders. In no time you will have built a fantastic treasure chest of usable ideas. Believe me, this will be one of the most nourishing things you can do for yourself and your creativity.

A small notebook in your purse will do the same job for you. I have many notebooks in my office and they are a constant source of inspiration to me. Sometimes I am amazed at what good ideas I had; go ahead and amaze yourself.

✑ First thing in the morning ✑

It's amazing how many marvelous ideas you get when you wake up in the morning. In the half life between sleep and the dreaded getting out of the bed there is a wonderful time when your mind serves up the answers to many of the problems you went to bed with.

Clarity strikes for a few brief minutes before all the tasks and chores rush into your mind. Capture those ideas immediately. It's a wonderful idea to have a pen and a stack of cards beside the bed.

✑ Conferences ✑

When you go to conferences or any kind of development program, there is always a danger of being overwhelmed with ideas coming at you from the stage. You listen, say wow, that's a great idea, I must do that. Yet you capture very few of them in a way which leads to your acting on them. You can make it too difficult for yourself.

The answer is to have a set of cards with you and only write down the 'keeper ideas.' A keeper is a specific actionable idea. Note the kernel point succinctly and how you will use it in your life. You will leave the event with a small number of clearly defined action points rather than a folder of notes which you will never re-read.

✑ Capturing the will-of-the-wisp ideas ✑

In everyday life when you are at meetings, your subconscious mind is always working away on issues and, if you are open to ideas, something said in another context can spark a new idea for you. In the midst of work, you can lose it. It just slips away. Capture it on a card immediately.

✥ For writers, speakers ✥ and consultants

Clip anything and everything that relates to your subject and keep the clippings in your idea box. You are building up a vast resource to help you when you are stuck for a new idea.

At the initial stages of researching any topic, you have clarity and a detachment before you begin to absorb large amounts of information. Your mind has a questioning detachment before it goes into the stage of sorting and absorbing facts and opinions. I always use my ideas box at this stage. I find that questions pop up, sometimes in no particular order. It is just my mind firing off questions. I note them down and use them later to crack open masses of information. The initial ideas are often the best.

✥ New job ✥

When you start a new job you have a rare few weeks when everything is new to you. You are too new to be held responsible for past decisions and actions. Treasure this time. Use your outsider perspective to really question everything. Record your questions. Capture your observations.

This time of detached clarity passes and soon you are forced into explanatory or, worse, defensive mode. If you have noted your initial observations down and your thoughts on what should be done these will be a very valuable resource for you. They act like a beacon of clear light. I always advise new appointees to do this.

✎ Kick start creativity ✎

One of the cornerstones of generating creativity is to leave your narrow niche or domain and to fill your mind with information and images from a completely different area. This shocks your brain and feeds it completely new material to work on.

That's why it is very good for artists to read the Financial Times and for bankers to visit art galleries. You get fantastic new insights and you must note them down as they occur to you.

✎ Vacations ✎

Have you noticed that when you go on vacation and switch off, your brain slowly lets go of the everyday lists and tasks? For some of us, it takes a few days before the brain lets go; for others, the mere sight of the airport does it. Whichever it is, you must realise that this can happen and let go. The very best ideas come when your brain relaxes.

I can't tell you how many busy executives have confirmed to me that they get their best ideas up mountains, on the beach, in the middle of swimming a length of a pool. The ideas come but you must grab them and record them. You can come back from a vacation with the most wonderful new perspectives.

Each action affects your Big Audacious Aim

Ask yourself this question before you undertake any action. 'Will this action take me towards achievement of my BAA – or take me away from it?'

If it moves you away, don't do it. This takes courage, so be selective and choose to move in the direction of your plan.

A clear attribute of every successful woman I have met is their ability to see their future in a crystal clear fashion. Furthermore, they crystalized this future into a clear aim. This aim was often quite awe inspiring and a little frightening. The fright got their adrenaline pumping. They usually had a Big Audacious Aim guiding them.

Career myopia

If you live totally in the present, you take a very short time perspective. You focus on what is in front of you. It can lead to career myopia. I hear women who suffer from this decrying that they find themselves lost in their career or even in their life. They don't understand what has happened to them.

If you want to be a really successful woman, stop living in the present. Successful women do not work from their present to their future. Remember this life changing concept – go to the future, see it, make your future in your future.

You can learn from very successful women

To really succeed you must also have your own Big Audacious Aim. When I ask women to fast forward to 10 years from now it has a profound affect upon them. They suddenly get serious and start concentrating.

You do it now. Count out 10 years. Focus on that date and decide where you want to be and what you want to be doing. This is the starting point for setting your future.

This is a good exercise because:

- It removes you from daily hassles.
- You move beyond the negatives.
- It opens up your mind to all possibilities.
- It gives you courage to dream.
- You take control of your business life.

Bridging the gap

A very simple first step is to realise that each action is taking you somewhere. Then you will know that every single action you take from now on has the potential to affect your progress towards your Big Audacious Aim.

Key question for you

Constantly ask yourself: Will this action take me closer to or further away from my Big Audacious Aim? Ask yourself this every evening as you plan the next day.

Ask yourself honestly if that meeting is essential or whether it is just you covering your ass. Do you need to take that course or do you already know enough? Are you doing the course because you are lacking the courage to actually do something? Be clear and don't substitute displacement activity for the key result-focussed activity.

It's up to you to step back and take the longer-term perspective. Make each action count. Why not? Going around in circles only makes you dizzy.

Take baby steps

Every step forward is important, even the baby ones. The important thing is that you are moving forward all the time.

Don't underestimate the positive effects of always progressing even if in imperceptible ways.

What is your next step?

Never underestimate the power of taking action rather than thinking about it. Taking any action means you are moving forward. Baby steps can be the most important steps you take.

I know many people who have wonderful dreams and yet never seem to achieve them. Sometimes it is because they fail to make a plan but more importantly it is because they become fearful or overwhelmed. They become inert and can't or won't take those first baby steps. I have had a number of very creative women on my SHOES program who suffer from inertia. It seems to particularly affect artistic people.

Taking the first step to your dream

Sara was a fantastic artist, working away in a room off her kitchen, painting in the evenings. She would come home from her day job as a draftswoman with a dream of being a successful painter who made her living from her art.

Sara was sabotaging herself in front of my eyes. Her work was clearly of the right standard but there was not enough of it to mount an exhibition to launch herself. She had no dedicated studio but worked in a communal family space. She had no goals and was not really making any progress towards her dream.

She was frustrated when she joined the program. It was clear to me that she needed to take a number of baby steps to escape from her inertia. So I challenged her to get a room somewhere out of the house, one that could be her studio.

I know how powerful that first set of baby steps can be in opening up the world of possibility to a trapped person. To my delight she turned up the next week with a space and to crown it all, we had the last session in her place surrounded by her paintings.

The next challenge was to mount an exhibition. So we agreed that the next baby step was to choose an artistic theme and to produce one painting. Believe it or not, she chose shoes as her theme.

Today, she has a number of exhibitions behind her and she's selling her paintings at a great price. Moreover, she is well on her way to doing it full time. For Sara, it all began with those first baby steps.

✎ Getting out of your way ✎
in one bound

Another artist I worked with wanted to change the way art was being taught in schools. She wanted it to be taken more seriously and decided she would take on this challenge. She was capable of succeeding but first she needed some credentials so that the 'powers that be' would really listen to her.

She knew she needed to be recognized in the academic world where the power to change rested. Although she was well qualified, she felt she needed higher qualifications, like a Masters in Education. Yet each year was passing and she was still chipping away, but not really making progress towards her major objective.

The baby step missing was finding the college she wanted to apply to and getting the necessary paperwork. It was such a small step yet one laden with serious consequences. She did it and has now almost finished her degree. The topic for her thesis is about improvements in methods of teaching art in schools.

Remember, the first baby steps can be the hardest in your mind but really make you feel great when you take them.

Are you stuck?

If you want to move job or need a job and are stuck, you can become depressed and lose energy. Here are the baby steps.

First you must see what is available. Don't think of this as a huge task. Break it into baby steps:

- Search online
- Buy newspapers
- Go to recruitment agencies

When you are stuck, you must remember it is not the actual step that is important, it is that you have begun moving again. You are tackling the inertia. So choose an easy first baby step.

What will be your first baby step?

Are you thinking of some steps you might like to take to move things along? If so, here's what to do. Get a notebook and write down the baby steps. Now take the first step. Make a big ceremony out of crossing it off.

You need to reward yourself for taking action! Good luck.

Everything you ever wanted is on the other side of fear

Fear is a paralyzing force stopping you moving forward or going out of your comfort zone.

Replace the fearful mindset with one which asks 'What is on the other side of fear?' and 'What will I gain if I move past it?'

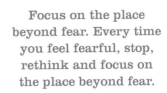

Focus on the place beyond fear. Every time you feel fearful, stop, rethink and focus on the place beyond fear.

Are you a serial procrastinator? If you are, then fear probably plays a big part in your life. Working with women all over the world has convinced me that fear knows no boundaries or cultural divides. At the heart of everyone is a core of fear. The main issue is how big that fear is, how you are coping with it and whether you have strategies for getting on despite the fears.

Not surprisingly, we are all afraid of different things. Other people's fears may seem tame compared to yours, but for everyone their fear can be a paralysing force in their lives causing them not to do certain things. I am very aware of this and look back and see where pure fear stopped me in my tracks. Yet I know it is possible to get beyond it.

⌘ My Sarajevo aha moment ⌘

A number of years ago I was asked to go and work in Bosnia Herzegovina to help rebuild the national development organizations. The country was getting ready to apply for and receive a huge amount of European Community funds. They needed to build the capacity of national organizations to handle this. My expertise was in building this kind of capacity in development organizations.

Yet right after I agreed to go, I realised I was scared about what I had landed myself in. I was going into a country which had been bitterly divided. It had just undergone a brutal civil war, and I was to be working through an interpreter – and all at five degrees farenheit!

I remember looking out the window of the plane as we flew over the rim of mountains, into the flat, saucer-like landscape which surrounds Sarajevo, the rim which made it easy for the snipers to keep Sarajevo under siege from April 1992 to February 1996.

❧ Going beyond my comfort zone ❧

I remember landing in the snow and driving into the city past all the bombed buildings, the bullet holes in every building and the signs of years of neglect. I looked out the hotel window at the overflowing cemetery on the hill. I sat down and said to myself, "What can you teach these people who have been through so much?" I was full of doubt and fear at that moment in time.

Have you felt like that? Not in Sarajevo but in a time or place where you knew you were about to go seriously beyond your comfort zone.

I went on to do three assignments there with my good friends John and Nadja. It was one of the most important experiences in my professional life. The fear was real but the overcoming of it was also real. I learnt a wonderful saying in Bosnia. It is "When the shoe fits, put a stone in it."

The main lesson I learnt there was that when you face up to your fear you often do your best work. You reach into your resources and find something else, often better stuff. This came home to me on the last day of one of my trips. I was asked to speak to the entire group in a final session to wrap everything up.

I had been working non-stop for 14 days and really felt that I had nothing worthwhile left to say. I thought I had told them everything I knew. So instead of standing at the top of the room I sat down in the group and said to them that I couldn't say anymore but that I would love to answer questions about all our work together and how they felt they could now implement it.

I will never forget what happened in the session. They asked questions and I answered them, drawing on all my experiences both good and bad. I told them about the biggest mistakes I had made as a CEO, my failures and a lot of the setbacks we had seen over the years.

I was unprepared for what happened. The silence was like velvet. I had their rapt attention. They were totally absorbed by one of the European experts sitting down and talking about fear and failure and what a life-changing teacher it can be.

I got a standing ovation for what I had done when I faced my fear, when I went totally outside my comfort zone and was myself.

So my learning was that you can amaze yourself by going through fear, without knowing what will be on the other side. In my mind, when faced with a difficult moment, I recall what I fondly christened "my Sarajevo moment" and say to myself, "you're afraid – but do it anyway".

✎ Make your own notes ✎

Believe in yourself

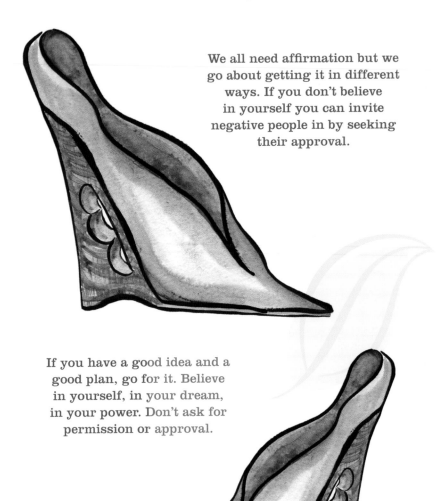

We all need affirmation but we go about getting it in different ways. If you don't believe in yourself you can invite negative people in by seeking their approval.

If you have a good idea and a good plan, go for it. Believe in yourself, in your dream, in your power. Don't ask for permission or approval.

☙ The power of self belief ❧

Self belief is at the base of your whole life. It is one of your most important assets. I have seen women with incredible self belief and a single idea become millionaires and the distinguishing factor was their unshakeable self belief. No matter how many times they were rejected their self belief was so strong that they kept on going.

I have also seen very talented women with lots of ideas squander their talents flitting from one idea to the next because they had no self belief. They did not really believe in their own talents and when they were disappointed they moved to another idea thinking that would help. Unfortunately, the one common denominator was themselves.

☙ Nurture self belief in your children ❧

We have a responsibility to build this self belief in our children. I see mothers all around me donating their life's blood to their children and yet still missing this vital ingredient. They drive them all over the city to classes, tutorials, football matches, all day and all weekend.

Their children have to learn music, dancing, sports and drama. These things must be accomplished! However, the core element of self belief can be missed. The core feeling they have about themselves can be trampled in the rush to gain accomplishments.

No time is given to sitting with the child, going at the child's pace, building up their confidence. I know one woman who spends more of her afternoons and evenings on the road in her car, ferrying them around, than she does at home with them. What message does that send to her children? If only they achieve all these skills they will be good enough – definitely not a good message.

✎ My wonderful dad ✎

One of my earliest memories of my dad was his constant refrain 'to be confident as other people take you at your own estimation.' When I was in school I was on the school debating team and used to get very nervous before each debate.

My dad was my biggest fan (my only one!) as well as my coach. Before each event my dad would say to me, "They are looking at you and taking their cue from you. They will think well of you if you think well of yourself."

Years later I was reminded of this very powerfully at the National Speakers Association annual convention in Orlando, Florida, when one of the top speakers told us that if you are on the stage and you look as though you are enjoying yourself the audience will believe you and start to enjoy themselves. In fact, he was saying they will take you at your estimation of yourself. It was the same thought after a gap of 35 years.

I love Eleanor Roosevelt's quote, which concisely reflects my dad's: "No one can make you feel inferior without your consent."

My dad never read a self-help book in his life. He was born in 1910 and died in 1997. He was a very wise man and he gave me that gold nugget of wisdom for life. Unfortunately, it's easy to accept that point intellectually but a life's work to make it integral to your life. I now realise that probably one of the most important things that a parent can do for a child is to give them confidence and make them think a lot of themselves.

❧ Don't confuse self belief ❧ with self confidence

Remember the crucial difference between self belief and self confidence. One is on the inside and is at your core, it is your inner self belief. It is a vital part of you and shines out from the center. It means you control your world from your inner being. This is a precious commodity. Guard it jealously.

Self confidence is another thing. You can project self confidence but still have little or no inner self esteem. Self confidence can be conjured up and projected like a halogen beam. The perfect combination is to have the two, but don't forget which is the core one.

❧ Make your own notes ❧

Abandon the twin fears

As we build our careers or our businesses, we feel fear. Some of us are afraid of failure, others of success and of shining too brightly. You will always get those thoughts.

From now on, identify them, isolate them, and quarantine them. Leave them there. Stop carrying them around with you.

There is a pair of terrible twins out there ready to get you. They are FEAR OF FAILURE and FEAR OF SUCCESS. Every woman's group I have ever worked with points to these two as the biggest obstacles towards women's success. They are the major fears suffered by the women I have worked with.

See if these resonate with you. Also look at the solutions we have come up with for each of them. Let me know if you come up with your own answers.

 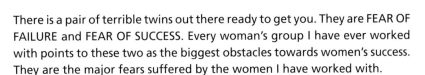

Top fears of failure

1. The fear: I won't do it right

Inside all of us is a little perfectionist trying to get out. Believe me it's in everyone.

In some people it is their driving force. This fear is that you won't be able to do it just right and it arises just when you are asked to do something larger or more daring than usual, something like make a presentation to your bosses, address a school board, or write a marketing plan or an annual report.

You have probably done something similar before, probably successfully, but the initial reaction can still be raw fear. I won't do it right! No way, I can't!

The answer: Yes you will

Do it anyway. Usually, your good is equivalent to most other's excellent. So believe in yourself and your ability. Most women who overcame this fear said that they found when they did things in their own unique way it always worked for them. Problems arose when they tried to imitate someone else's style or content.

❧ Top fears of failure ❧

2. The fear: I am not good enough

I wonder if this is a problem of our conditioning as women. In constantly telling us to be humble, is it possible that our parents may have set us up for an overdose of self doubt? I constantly come across women who are outwardly very confident but inwardly feel they are not good enough.

The answer: Yes you are

You are good enough and better than most. Many women have said to me that they found the answer in banning negative thoughts and in actively seeking out things they could be proud of. They had a positive plan to be self nourishing, constantly addressing the fear with self affirmations.

3. The fear: What will others think of me?

People are either self referencing or other referencing. Self referencing people look inside themselves for guidance and approval; other referencing people look outside themselves to others and take their guidance and approval from them. This fear can be very real for other referencing people. They are constantly scanning the room to see what others think of them.

The answer: Think first of yourself

Think first of your own opinion of yourself. Put the opinion of others in perspective. Women have told me that they escaped from this fear by dividing people into two. The first group were people whose opinion they rated. They listened to constructive comments from them. The second group were people whose opinion they did not rate, either because they were not sufficiently qualified to comment or they suspected the motives of the person.

4. The fear: There are too many challenges to me doing this

I have seen women becoming paralysed by fear because they cannot see through to the final task but can only see the problems and obstacles along the way. They are playing safe by pointing out all that can go wrong, in the belief that if is does they are safe as they can say, "I told you it wouldn't work."

The answer: Yes but do it anyway

Let's face it, there are always challenges. Anything worth doing is not going to be easy. If it was it would already be done. A really good way to sort out the real obstacles from the imaginary ones is to use the three-part flipchart method. Divide a flipchart or a sheet of paper or into three columns as follows:

- Easily doable points
- Challenges/difficulties
- Interesting points

This allows you to develop perspective by making the challenges only one third of the discussion. Putting a potential challenge into the interesting column allows for open discussion.

❧ Top fears of success ❧

1. The fear: I will reveal too much of myself if I get all that attention

I have seen women quail at the thought of bringing attention to themselves. They have a realistic view of themselves and know if they go for promotion they will get it, but fear of being noticed stops them.

The answer: No you won't

This is a tricky one. Women tell me it is often a problem of self worth that inhibits their progress. They feel unworthy of any 'higher' position. The solution is to slowly build their confidence until they feel comfortable with any attention.

2. The fear: I will shine too brightly

Some women know they are capable of great things. They have innate gifts, which make them potentially the leaders in our society. Yet somewhere in their conditioning, they absorbed the idea that you must not draw attention to yourself. The phrases "who do you think you are?" or "what makes you think you can do that?" echo in their heads.

The answer: Think carefully

To escape this kind of conditioning you first have to realise that you are conditioned. Some women fail to realise that they have completely swallowed the values and norms of a different age. They are not questioning their automatic thoughts or fears. I have seen women transformed when they realise that they are being controlled by invisible puppet strings operated by words spoken twenty years previously.

3. The fear: I won't be able to sustain the performance

They think 'I am good enough to win that election but once I have the position I will be found out. I am good enough to get it but then what?" You can witness amazing acts of self sabotage by women who think like this. They scupper their own winning strategies because of their own fear. Sadly, they often do it subconsciously, making it harder to address and put an end to such thoughts.

The answer: Take each fear as it comes

The answer lies in taking each fear as it comes. No one can control the outcomes of the future. You don't know the inner resources you have or what you can do if you are under pressure. Again the problem lies in self belief. I tell women to realistically and impersonally evaluate their opposition. They need to see that they are as good as anyone so why not take a chance on themselves? They could stun themselves!

Change your thoughts

Your thoughts are the basis of everything. Thought comes first, then action. Every day, we have more than 20,000 thoughts which surface to our consciousness.

From these, we can often focus on problems and fears. This keeps us looking at the half empty glass. Change those thoughts. Make more of them positive and make them work to move you forward.

✏ Practice conscious thinking ✏

Practice conscious thinking. Stop and think. Yes, think. Your thoughts are at the start of everything. The thought comes first then the decision and then the actions.

I urge you to spend more time really examining your thoughts and your thought patterns. Too much of our thoughts today come in a lazy way. We allow other people to think for us. Look at the media, newspapers and television. How much do you question what they are telling you? How much do you consciously work out for yourself? Resolve to question everything you are told, don't accept it as the absolute truth, work it out for yourself.

Try not to be unconscious when you are awake! Challenge your thoughts about yourself. Your view of yourself is vital to how successful you will be. Have you ever questioned how the current view you have came about? Did you decide on this view recently or is it one you formed 10-20 years ago? Change these thoughts. If you think you are not good enough then question where this thought came from. Is it based on a fact? If so, what fact? Is this still relevant?

✏ Find out how others view you ✏

On my SHOES program we always start with an exercise where the women actively ask others for their view of them and their unique gifts. Knowing this can have the most profound effect on you.

We can fear what others think of us. We are usually wrong, as they think a lot more of us than we realize, but we rarely give them an opportunity to tell us.

I am now giving you the chance to do this exercise. You will be thrilled at what a positive confidence-building exercise this is.

ᘐᕐ Who do you ask? ᕐᘐ

It is simple. You ask trusted positive people what they think of you, particularly your unique attributes.

Rules

ᘐᕐ Only ask positive people (you have enough of your own negative thoughts)

ᘐᕐ Only ask people whose opinion you rate (Why ask an idiot to give you feedback?)

ᘐᕐ Only ask people who care about you and mean you well (Why invite negative, hurtful people into your inner space?)

Often people ask their partner and while that can be useful I suggest you be brave and go ask customers, colleagues, and employees.

ᘐᕐ What do you ask? ᕐᘐ

You tell them you are undertaking an exercise to build up your self esteem in your business. You are doing an audit of your assets – the biggest one being you. You are looking for a golden nugget, an insight that will greatly encourage you.

ᘐᕐ How do you do it? ᕐᘐ

Be very businesslike about this and choose your person carefully. Explain it in detail and give them a written request. Ask them to give you a written reply. Give them a few days to do it, no more. Ask for the returned document on a specific day. This way you have set them up to do it seriously and, believe me, if you do this set up correctly you will get serious and insightful replies.

Challenge problem-focused thinking

I see women who when you present them with a new idea they always think of the problems first. They can't help themselves. They go straight past the excitement to seeing the obstacles, drawbacks and worst-case scenario. While this kind of thinking has its place in the world, to stop the over-positive types running riot, I urge you to consider if you are doing this.

If so, stop. Practice the following

- Listen…really listen until the whole idea is explained.
- Breathe deeply. Wait. Keep waiting.
- Watch the other person. Read their body language. Have they just shared a life's dream with you?
- Pause when you hear a new idea and force yourself to look at the positives.
- Note the positive aspects only.

How often are you inclined to do this? Do you greet each new idea with caution? Does your thinking default to worry mode because that is the way it has always been?

Know your hotspots and control them

Observe yourself. Know what triggers your annoyance or anger. These are your hot spots. If someone's behavior or words touches a hot spot it triggers your hostile reaction.

Letting people control you in this way gives them control over your behavior. Take control back. What hot spot will you cool first?

Every one of us has hot spots. You know what they are when someone presses them and you overreact, often before you have time to think. They hit the spot and you react, it's over in the blink of an eye.

Believe me, everyone around you, especially your family, knows your hotspots. It's a sad situation if you don't know them. You leave yourself wide open to manipulation as people know exactly which action or word will affect and excite you. They can control your behavior.

ᕦ Hotspots are triggered in two ways. ᕤ Trigger phrases and trigger situations

Trigger phrases

Here are some red hot trigger phrases. Do you relate to any of these?

- ᕦ I think you could have done a better job.
- ᕦ I would not have done it like that.
- ᕦ Why can't you understand?
- ᕦ I am disappointed in you.
- ᕦ I expected more.
- ᕦ Where have you been?
- ᕦ Don't do it like that.
- ᕦ You are no good at that.
- ᕦ It's the best I can do.

Have you got your own? What are they?

Why are phrases like these making you mad? Have you thought about it? Can you remember a situation where you reacted before you even realised it? Usually these phrases trigger something deeper, some other experience where you were annoyed or put down. This phrase acts like a lightening rod bringing it all back. The key point is the power of the trigger and how it affects the speed with which you react. The answer lies in controlling the trigger, preferably in turning it off.

✐ The work for you ✐

Listen more

You have to start listening to what people say to you – really listening. This means pausing, breathing slowly and watching the other person while giving them time to say what they have to say. Be careful not to listen only with your ears. Work for total listening which comes when you read the facial expressions, the gesticulations, the movement, the level of threat and the energy levels. It is essential to read all of these to get a full understanding of what the person means.

When you hear your trigger phrases you will know you need:

✐ To deepen your listening

✐ To give the other person the benefit of the doubt

✐ To allow yourself time to control your reactions

Reframe the phrase

When you think someone has said something that sets you off, take a moment and totally reframe the sentence. For example, if someone says, **"Why do you always do it like that?"** pause and think before reacting. You might immediately think that they are criticising you. However, if you try reframing it as follows see what happens to your thinking.

They could mean; **"I am impressed with your results and I wonder is there a reason that you decided to always do it like that."**

"I always try doing it in different ways so I wonder why you always do it like that."

Do you see if you reframe and look at the question from different angles you can change the emphasis and often take the sting out of the question?

Trigger Situations

There are certain situations which make you uncomfortable and set you up to be on edge and therefore prone to overreaction.

Do any of these situations echo with you?

- You feel you are doing everything for someone but they never show you any appreciation.
- You feel you are doing the best you can and still people are finding fault.
- You are working very hard and still more is expected.
- You feel that your male boss is treating the male employees better, taking them to play golf but when you want time off for a personal problem, like a sick child, it's frowned upon.

Think of your own examples. Are there situations which set you off?

Here are the first steps to solve this. Look at the situation in a detached way as if it was happening to someone else. Take all the emotion out of it. Be rational and then apply all your coping strategies to it. Remove its irrational hold over you.

Regain control. Which hot spot will you cool first?

Even when you fall, you fall forward

Don't let fear of making a mistake and falling down stop you. Think of mistakes as a way to learn lessons. Mistakes are the best teachers.

Don't waste energy on self doubt. You do your best, you give your essence, you try to please others and then you doubt if you are good enough. Stop doubting yourself – it serves no purpose. It saps your energy. Move on in a positive frame of mind.

Never be afraid of doing something because you think you might make a mistake. Don't let the fear of appearing stupid and falling down stop you doing things. Think of mistakes as a learning process. Mistakes are the best teachers. The more mistakes you make the more you learn.

I would prefer you to be trying out lots of ideas and learning as you go along, rather than doing nothing and waiting for perfection.

The best lesson

I always remember the time I really internalized this lesson. I was on maternity leave from my job as CEO of a major health not for profit organization and I was due back at work the next week.

I was near the office with my baby son and had decided to call in to introduce him and make final arrangements for the following week. I had kept in close contact with the office but I had not been into the building in person.

I walked in, unannounced, to find the hall and all the stairs packed up with boxes of literature. This was not what I expected. I found one of my staff and her expression told me she was shocked to see me.

I discovered she had made a mistake in the numbers on the order paperwork for the new newsletter and this meant we had just ordered 5,000 more than we needed. This was a big spend and clearly a non-returnable one.

What would you have done? This was a fantastic worker who had made a genuine mistake, mainly due to her enthusiasm. Should the mistake have been used against her? I decided to let this mistake be our biggest investment in staff learning and development that year.

We changed our procedures so it would not happen again. We came up with a very creative way of using the surplus copies in a promotional campaign and we all learnt a big lesson. I know that woman will never make a mistake like that again. So we all fell forward and no one died!

 When did you learn from a mistake?

Sit down and think. Can you recall a time you learnt a big lesson from a mistake? If not, look at some of your biggest mistakes and reframe them looking for potential lessons as you do so.

Powerful leadership tool

This is a powerful tool in leadership. When people realize that you are not operating a blame culture, but a learning one, they feel freer to experiment and innovate. How many companies have you seen give a mixed message to staff? One message says we are leaders in customer service, we aim to please.

The contradictory message is do everything exactly as we say in the manuals. Sadly, customers rarely fit into the procedures outlined in manuals. So what is the result of the mixed signal? When the employee steps out of the box to solve the customer's unique problem they are chastised for not following procedures.

What does the staff learn? They quickly learn that taking the initiative means making a mistake and mistakes are not tolerated. This is a blame culture in full stride.

Don't waste energy on self doubt

Don't let your fear of making a mistake fill you with self doubt. I don't suggest that you become utterly reckless, but I do recommend that when you are doubtful you choose action over inaction and see what happens.

Self doubt can be a corroding force in your life. It can sap your energy little by little. We are all afraid of appearing foolish but we rarely do. Sometimes we think people are paying us attention and it can be a wake up call to realize most people are so self-absorbed that they are impervious to you and your 'mistakes.'

You do your best, you give your essence, you try to please others and then you doubt if you are good enough. Stop doubting yourself – it serves no purpose. It saps your energy.

✎ Turning a mistake into a golden ✎ nugget for a customer

Taking a mistake and turning it around allows you to exceed everyone's expectations. A tailor I know prides himself on his customer service and encourages his staff to do whatever is required to please customers.

One New Year a large gent came in to get specially fitted dress shirts. All went well and the man left. The shirts were made and posted to the address several hundreds miles away.

They arrived the day before his New Year's Eve gala dinner and the man phoned, angrily claiming they were too small. They had posted the wrong ones. My friend, who is a firm believer in the school of turning problems into opportunities, said to the large gent that all would be well. Just leave it with me, he said.

So he sent the junior tailor by car to personally deliver the shirts and a free set of cufflinks. What was the result? That salesman never made that mistake again and the gent sings my friend's praises everywhere he goes!

So go make lots of mistakes and reap the benefits of a good education!

End each week by making your plan for the following week

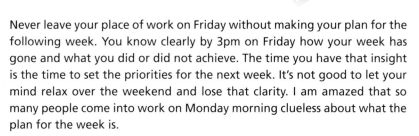

On Friday, set out your principal goals for the following week.

That way, you start Monday morning organized. Take an overview of the week and plan your activities for each day so that you reach your goals for the week by Friday.

Never leave your place of work on Friday without making your plan for the following week. You know clearly by 3pm on Friday how your week has gone and what you did or did not achieve. The time you have that insight is the time to set the priorities for the next week. It's not good to let your mind relax over the weekend and lose that clarity. I am amazed that so many people come into work on Monday morning clueless about what the plan for the week is.

Do you do this? Does this sound familiar? Monday morning comes and you go to work and you look at your desk and say, "What now?" Is that when you go get coffee? Do you check every email you got? Do you then answer every email, even the obvious garbage?

This is displacement activity, which we all engage in when we have lost our focus. You can eliminate this by simply starting the week on the previous Friday at 3pm.

First you should take a week-long view, as making detailed plans for each day, in the absence of a weekly plan, is less effective.

Decide on the top three goals for the week. Make them the goals which you simply must accomplish. You have a far greater chance of realizing them than if you give yourself a huge list.

Start on Monday morning with your number one goal. Go straight for it. That way you have a sense of purpose when you hit the door and you eliminate all the usual time-wasting, waffly activities. You also give most of your energy to your top priority goals. This is much better than working on minor items at the beginning of the week and slowly working up to the priorities.

Make each action count

Make a list of your goals. Put a completion date after each goal. Sub-divide each goal into the actions needed to achieve the goal. Look at the completion date of the goal and slot the actions into the days from now until then. Move everything around until you have all the actions in before the end date. Put these in your diary. This means you'll be prioritising the actions linked to your goals and not on random actions like compulsively checking emails.

Principles for instant productivity

You can hugely increase your productivity with a number of simple work practices.

1. Review your progress in achieving your actions in the week gone by. Did you get all the scheduled ones done? If not readjust next week to absorb them.

2. Make your weekly plan before you leave work on Friday.

3. Have a daily and weekly planner.

4. Set weekly goals first.

5. Prioritise them into:

   a. Must do
   b. Nice to do
   c. Icing on the cake

6. Have firm weekly goals but more flexible daily action lists.

7. Have a separate long-range master to-do list from which you draw the weekly goals.

Until now

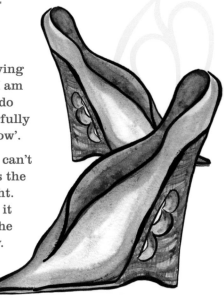

When you find yourself saying self-defeating things like 'I am useless at this' or 'I can't do that', stop and use a wonderfully liberating phrase –'until now'.

So the thought changes to 'I can't do that...until now'. It stops the negative stream of thought. Use it all the time and let it go to work on reducing the unquestioned negativity.

Have you found yourself using self-limiting phrases where you actually put a limit on your own performance? Have you stopped yourself doing things? Do these phrases sound familiar? "I have never been able to start my own business," or "I keep trying to get a better job."

Do you really listen to your self chatter, the constant conversations we have with ourselves. If not, tune in more carefully. Listen and note down your most common phrases.

It is even better when you ask a trusted person to listen carefully and note your explanations or excuses for inaction. It is especially important to do this now as we really need to do everything to stay positive and empowered.

You may not even be aware of your self talk. I find that when women first come to my SHOES program they often say very self-defeating things. A common one is, "I have been unable to break free, to do what I really want to do," or "I am finding it impossible to keep the business going."

☙ Listen to your self talk ❧

In the group, when everyone is focused on their future, you begin to listen keenly to the phrases others repeat. The pattern of their thoughts can very quickly become clear in an environment like that. An observant listener can tune in accurately to your self talk in a few minutes. Imagine the insights when a group of observant women focus on you.

☙ Two magic phrases ❧

A powerful tool is to reframe these self-defeating phrases. I find that there are two phrases that are very powerful in helping you do this: "Until now" and "from now on."

Until now

The first magic phrase is "until now" It helps you break your self defeating thought patterns. Have you noticed lately how we are all sliding into a similar viewpoint? It goes like this, times are tough, business is hard, I can't seem to get the results I used to, and I feel worn out. You can use "until now" to break that pattern.

When I hear the phrase "I have been unable to go out and get new business," I always say to them, "until now." Then I encourage them to repeat it so they reframe and say, "Until now, I have been unable to go out and get new business."

As you can imagine, this has a powerful effect. It stops the thought pattern and removes its control over you. It allows you to question, for example, am I really paralysed? If you keep reframing the negative thoughts you can reorientate yourself completely. You just don't let your thoughts settle into a self defeating pattern.

Try this yourself. Examine your explanations for your actions or inactions. Constantly add the magic phrase. See how it makes you rethink things.

From now on

The second magic phrase is "from now on."

After you have said "until now" you start the next sentence with "from now on." This moves you forward and opens up the possibility of your deciding on an alternative future direction. You allow yourself to take control of the future.

So we are now saying, "Until now, I have been unable to do what I really want, but from now on I will do what I want to do."

By this simple exercise you can stop your repeat thinking. It is a really effective tool. It stops you short. Use it on people. You can get them to see what is a past thought and that they can reframe it.

If you are part of a group, a team or a committee, which is always thinking of problems and loves a negative approach you can introduce this tool.

We are surrounded by people who make assumptions. They assume that because it didn't work in the past it won't work in the future. Using these tools forces them to re-evaluate and think harder.

Once you make it clear that every stated assumption is going to be met with an "until now" they quickly realize that they will not get away with lazy thinking.

They will have to look at alternative scenarios. After a number of sessions you will find everyone in the room is using it and quickly the positive energy starts to flow. It opens up possibilities.

✌ Recession beaters ✌

It's time to buck up and use whatever tools you have to counteract the gloom that can over take you. Try the following as a quick booster.

My self defeating thought	Change to "Until now"	Add "From now on"
1.		
2.		
3.		
4.		
5.		

If you are having difficulty doing this on your own I suggest that you gather a group of trusted women around you, and after you have studied the Shoeism, and tried it individually, that you do the exercise together. Help each other until you have a wonderfully tuned approach to reframing all your self limiting thoughts.

A wonderful benefit of doing this with a group of people you spend time with is that you can reframe each others thoughts. You can banish self limiting thoughts and phrases from each others heads.

You may not have done this until now ....from now on make it a part of your life!

Act like a tortoise

When you are facing a challenge, don't ask for permission to act. If you know you are correct stick your neck out of your tortoise shell and go for it. You can always ruminate over it all later.

Remember success favors the courageous.

I studied zoology in college and have retained a life long fascination with animals and especially the lessons we can learn from them. I really love tortoises and wonder at their survival. I find their lifestyle and survival mechanisms are very interesting and a great metaphor for learning.

There are two principal lessons I have drawn from them over the years. The first is slow and steady wins the race, the second is when you are facing a challenge, don't ask for permission to act. If you know you are correct stick your neck out of your shell and go for it. I feel we can take the lessons and apply them to our lives.

∼ The hare and the tortoise: ∼ slow and steady wins the race

My fascination with tortoises began in childhood with Aesop's famous fable about the Hare and the Tortoise. Aesop's fables are a source of enormous wisdom and entertainment. Each fable always ends with a moral, usually a point of eminent good sense.

Here is a short version of the Hare and the Tortoise:

The hare ridicules the slow pace and short feet of the tortoise. So the tortoise challenges him to a race saying he can beat him. The fox chooses the course and sets the goals. On the day of the race the tortoise sets off, crawling at his usual steady pace, not stopping at all.

The hare shoots off and once he reaches the middle point he stops, begins eating grass, lying in the sun and relaxing. He nods off to sleep. He is certain he will easily outrun the tortoise. Even if the tortoise gets ahead he feels he can fly right by him.

In the meantime the tortoise just plods along straight to the finishing line. When the hare wakes up he is all alone, and cannot see his opponent. So he heads for the finish as fast as he can. As he runs across the line he is surprised to see the tortoise has already crossed it and is waiting patiently for him.

ᴗ Only compete with yourself ᴗ

So the moral is: slow and steady wins the race. I always recommend this story to people in a corporate setting. You can get dazzled by high fliers all around you at work. They seem to be hanging out with the leaders, always on trips, always making presentations that land huge clients. Or so it can seem, especially if you fall for the hare's own propaganda!

I recommend that you should not compete with the hares but instead compete with yourself. You set your own goals and your own standards. I have seen a lot of burnt-out corporate hares in my time and I am never impressed by flamboyant hare behavior.

The next time you feel yourself getting overwhelmed by a 'long eared' colleague think of the tortoise.

ᴗ Be a tortoise, don't ask ᴗ
for permission to act

One of the things that drives me crazy is when someone has a great idea, has done their research and knows it will succeed – but still won't act because they feel they need permission first. They feel some need for advance approval before they act. In today's fast moving world of business, this approach can lose you money.

I worked with a woman who had a small business and she had the opportunity to supply an expanding company with her product. She was a main provider of that product in the area but felt she should wait and check with the manufacturer in case she stepped on someone's toes.

Guess what, when she did not act they phoned her competitor who delivered immediately and took the business out from under her nose. She should have stuck her neck out of her shell! She was aghast at what happened and learnt her lesson. She is now one of my bravest tortoises. There is nothing like a sharp knock on your shell to wake you up.

The bottom line is that success favors the courageous. So take action, you can always ruminate over it all later.

🐾 Hares panic, tortoises win 🐾

In times of difficulty in our lives we often find ourselves torn between paralysing fear, unable to do anything and panicky fear where we allow our panic to propel us into action.

I am seeing a lot more of the panicky hopping behavior of hares at the moment. There is a general climate of panic fuelled by fear in the small business community and people are rushing into all kinds of activities without sufficient thought. I suggest that you don't confuse reactive panicky actions with business planning.

Think twice before slashing prices, printing thousands of flyers, dropping services, letting staff go, and changing your way of doing business. Stop and think carefully.

🐾 Any hare activities? 🐾

Let's do something very practical to help you enact this Shoeism. Have a good think and list the top five challenges facing you right now. Write them down in the table below and then list the responses you are thinking about making. When you have done that, take the next step and categorise your response as a hasty hare or thoughtful tortoise. Use this exercise to calm your panicky hare.

Top 4 Challenges	Responses	Hasty hare response?	Thoughtful tortoise response?

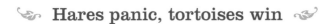

Write morning pages

Every morning, start your day
with three pages of writing in your
morning page journal. You will never
get a better insight into your own
mind and its workings.

Write from the heart – with no editing.
Let it flow from your head, down
your arm and onto the page, with no
negative editing or checking.

✍ Why first thing in the morning? ✍

The very best and easiest way to access your subconscious mind is to write every morning. Buy yourself a notebook and pen and put them beside your bed. Every morning when you open your eyes get out of bed and start writing. You will be amazed at what insights you uncover.

When you go to bed you put all your questions and worries to bed as well. Except your subconscious mind does not join you in sleep, it keeps working away on your concerns. So first thing in the morning you get a rare insight into what your subconscious has been working on. If you tap straight into it with freestyle writing you can capture what is on the top of your subconscious mind. A rare insight!

Now let's deal with the problems you may have with this:

- ✍ I don't have time.
- ✍ I can't write.
- ✍ I don't know what to write.
- ✍ I think this is too self-indulgent.
- ✍ My family will think I have gone mad!
- ✍ I don't want to know what is going on in there.

All of these are excuses. Your family probably think you are mad anyway! There is no set way to write; no right, no wrong. You need to know what is going on in your own head.

❧ Getting a major insight ❧
into your mindset

Promise yourself you will write every morning for 21 days. You know that it takes 21 days to make or break a habit.

Write every morning but don't read what you have written. Wait for the 22nd day. By doing this you allow yourself to reveal what is on your mind without your editor being activated. Read the whole 21 days and see how often the same thought comes up. That will be a remarkable gift to you.

Celine, one of my SHOES women, was in the process of deciding whether to leave her present employer, a consultancy company, and set up her own company. She really wanted to do this but somehow kept putting off the day she would leave, even though she was ready to do so.

She had a brilliant set of qualifications, an excellent client list, and she was very well regarded in her profession. She was ready but ridden with doubts.

She started morning pages and asked herself, "Why am I reluctant to go out on my own?" She did the writing for three weeks without reading it. She kept asking why she was hesitating.

She discovered how often fear appeared in the writing. She had no idea how much her life was ruled by fear. It was like a low-running motor in the background – everything was affected by it. She told me that this was an incredible insight for her.

When she realised this she decided to go ahead and leave anyway. She knew the fear would remain, yet she could not let it dominate her. She realised that she would have to acknowledge it and work with it. Once she uncovered it, she was able to figure out what to do and so it lost its power over her.

Your early morning writing

- Trust yourself.
- Write early in the morning when you awake.
- Don't worry about your content.
- Ask yourself a question as you fall asleep.
- Answer it in your morning writing.
- Don't read it straight away – wait a number of weeks.
- Under no circumstances edit it.

Believe me, this is a very valuable tool – one of the most powerful you will ever come across.

You would be great if you got out of your own way

Discover how much of your failure to reach goals is due to your mindset. Your actions are preceded by thoughts which come from your mindset. So your most effective self development work is within your own head.

Clear away the negatives, the doubts, the self sabotage, and focus on the positive outcomes. Get out of your own way.

Find out how you are blocking yourself and put a stop to it

We are all capable of standing in our own way. We trap ourselves continuously. When I gave a keynote speech to a conference of Irishwomen working in the agricultural sector I felt they were so much in their own way I called the speech 'You would be great if you got out of your own way.'

❧ The Venus flytraps of life ❧

I talked to the women about the dangers of having life-gobbling fears in their lives. To make my point I told them about one of my favorite plants, the Venus flytrap.

It is a carnivorous plant which traps and eats insects and has leaves which act like a mouth, that open wide. On the leaves are short, stiff hairs called trigger hairs. When anything touches these hairs enough to bend them, the two lobes of the leaves snap shut trapping whatever is inside. The trap will shut in less than a second.

I suggested that women have their own private Venus flytraps in their lives. Flytraps they put in their path include fear of success, fear of failure, self-sabotage and allowing negative people to constantly drain them.

I was overwhelmed by the positive feedback that I received. It really touched a cord with the women. Many freely admitted to me that they had not realised until then that they were completely blocking themselves. They simply had not stood in their own power. They thought they were being actively blocked from outside, but in fact they were the blocks themselves.

The biggest block they had was not standing up and being counted. An economist working on generating information about Irish agriculture had written that there were more statistics about animals and land than about women in agriculture in Ireland. It was clear that these women needed to stand up and when they did so they would be formidable.

⋙ Always face up to reality ⋘ and then begin to deal with it

You stay in your own way by not facing up to reality. You can go through life without asking yourself any difficult questions. You can just float along or worse, struggle and never undergo any self discovery or self-examination. We stay in our own way when we never question ourselves, never explore beneath the surface of our lives.

You can say, "I don't have the tools to do that" but that is a cop out. The tools are all around you and the first tool is the easiest: ask questions. Never assume anything. In my courses, I always remind people that ASSUME makes an ASS out of U and ME.

I remember when I wanted to write and publish my first book. I had spoken about it for a long time but had done nothing. I moaned on and on and wished and wished until a friend of mine finally lost patience with me.

He challenged me by asking what was stopping me. You know the answer – myself. So he said to me, "Just do it – get out of your own way and do it." I was startled by this but did get out of my own way and my first book was published the following year.

Use your female intuition to get out of your own way

Most women I have ever met have intuition, but only a few trust it enough to use it.

Clearly there is a scale of intuition, ranging from little intuition through average intuition to high intuition. Very intuitive people can seem as though they have second sight. They have the ability to see the big picture, to connect disparate facts into a comprehensible picture and to be futuristic.

They make leaps of understanding and often don't know how they got to their new perception. It's like a gift and it needs nurturing. It boils down to the gut feeling you get about someone or something. The longer you live and the more experience you get the better your intuition. It is a constantly developing attribute.

Can we trust our intuition?

I completely trust this type of intuition, sometimes called your gut feeling. So why do women not trust it more? Do you trust your intuition? I can't tell you the number of women who say to me that they had a bad feeling about someone but they hired them anyway.

They were bedazzled by a fabulous resume but overlooked their gut feeling that the person was not going to fit into their company.

So if you are having difficulty getting going, always consult your intuitive self – it knows an awful lot more than you've ever imagined.

Summer

When I wrote these summer Shoeisms, I had a very specific intent in mind. I was thinking of summer as a time of flowering and plenty, a time when nature flourishes and bright colors are everywhere. It is a time when we relax, take time out and go on our vacation. We spend hours thriving in the warm sun and looking benignly on the world.

Every summer, my family goes to the beach and imbibes the sound of the waves. We collect shells, fish and look at the sunsets; this is the time when we feel we are thriving. We arrive worn out and slowly fill up with sunshine and go home feeling very optimistic and ready to aim for thriving again.

I wanted these Shoeisms to be as wonderful as that kind of a summer vacation for you, to allow you to have the thought provokers to allow you to experience the wonderful effect of a summer vacation.

We need to make a practice of thriving. This is vital now more than ever, as the easy thing to do today would be to hunker down and say that you hoped to survive the declining times and to be still around when recovery comes. That is the easy option and deeply unfulfilling in the long run.

❧ An opportunity to thrive ❧

I encourage you to look at the present difficulties in this exciting way – not as a time for survival but as a time for finding the opportunity to thrive. Do not succumb to the gloom-laden reports everywhere in the media as they will sap your will to live.

Instead, use these summer Shoeisms to take charge of your own thoughts and aspirations.

I want you to use them to focus on thriving, being future-orientated and achieving excellence. Move away from the survival mode and stand in the sun. Look for that sparkling thought or idea that comes with the brightness of summer thoughts. Go on – what have you to lose?

One of my favorite poets, Emily Dickinson, caught the idea of the magic of summer when she said

"A something in a summer's noon,
An azure depth, a wordless tune,
Transcending ecstasy.

And still within a summer's night
A something so transporting bright,
I clap my hands to see; "

From her poem,
A something in a summer's day

I hope these summer Shoeisms will help you to achieve that thriving feeling by introducing you to concepts like faking it until you make it, always looking forward, making your future in the future, and determining to thrive – not survive.

Fake it until you make it

You become your thoughts, so it is a major step to success to see your success clearly and then act as if you were that success. In effect, you conjure up your success …fake it and then segue into the reality of that success.

Embrace change

There is only one certainty after death and taxes – and that is change. You need to embrace it or be left far behind. Explore this concept and see how comfortable you are with integrating change into the fabric of your life.

Always look forward

The past is gone and it is pointless worrying about it. Instead, embrace the idea of being someone who always looks forward. Become a person of immense possibilities, always asking exploratory questions like 'what if?'.

Capture your ideas and write them down

Do yourself a favor and value your own genius. Realize that your ideas are as good as anyone's and capture them before they fade away into your busy life. Use the twenty tips to gather your own valuable thoughts.

Donate to the giant favor bank

There is a wondrous metaphor which opens up enormous possibilities. Imagine the world as one giant bank brimming full of people willing to help you. All you have to do to start withdrawing is to donate some unasked for favors to people, with no strings attached.

You make your future in your future

People who thrive are the ones who see their future with crystal clarity. Become one of them and be a future person. Learn the steps to living in the future and to morphing into a futurist.

Don't be merely successful – be significant

Pause and be clear on the difference between success and significance. Decide on the harder and more rewarding one and learn how to make a significance plan.

Make your message match the messenger

Incongruence is the easiest thing to spot and can fatally weaken your business image. You must examine the image you project and be totally consistent in the message.

Explore other domains

Make a deliberate plan to make curiosity a part of your life. Never get stuck in what you know – instead, go out and explore other areas of expertise. Grow better in meeting the intellectual challenge.

Act strategically to achieve you Big Audacious Aim

Wandering about aimlessly without a plan will result in random aimless results. Everyone can plan and if you really want to get to your life's aim, have a look at this succinct introduction to strategic planning.

Don't be a hoarder – let things go

Hoarding is the enemy of bright summer vibrations. Learn how to escape the trap of surrounding yourself with deadening ideas, people and possessions. Break out into the bare sunshine so you can move on.

Find the best and benchmark against them

You can never go wrong if you emulate the best. Discover the concept of personal benchmarking and incorporate it in to your successful life. The best hang out with the best.

Find your adult state

Clear thinking and adult behavior are essential for success. This simple thought will show you how to stay in productive detached mode more of the time. Banish your outer child!

Thrive not survive

This is one of the most powerful of the summer Shoeisms as it challenges you to go beyond the easy route of choosing to survive the current climate and asks you to actively thrive instead.

Fake it until you make it

If you have set yourself a goal to achieve something, then act as if you have already achieved it.

Live as if it is yours. If you want to be a successful businessperson then act like one. Speak like one. Dress like one. Fake it until you make it.

If you think you will succeed, you will. Soon it will be yours.

Do you feel that you can't quite pull it off and that the effort of being fabulous all the time is too much for you? Have you ever set yourself a huge target and then found yourself wilting under the pressure of achieving it?

❧ Bridge that gap ❧

This is the gap between what we wish for and what we are.

Everyone experiences this, even the most successful women. It can be exhausting projecting success all the time, so the best way to bridge the gap is to fake it until you make it.

I mean faking it in the best sense, of course!

❧ Go to the place of success ❧

Turn your mind to the place you want to be, whether it's giving a fantastic presentation, closing a big sale, or impressing the interview board. Then go there fully in your thoughts. Act as if you were already doing it successfully, with panache. You may be full of doubts, or feel tired or fed up. Ignore that.

Not everyone becomes a so-called overnight success – not literally overnight. Many 'overnight successes' will tell you it took them five to ten years. So it's important to believe in yourself and in your vision. You must believe that you are already successful, already living your vision.

You know you are going to make it, but you must be realistic – it takes time and lots of hard work. No amount of wishing for success will make you successful without the hard graft.

This Shoeism is to help you bridge the gap between your future dream and the reality of now. You must envision yourself clearly achieving it. How would you look, how would you behave, and what image would you be projecting? See yourself as successful. Now, begin to live and act like that today.

Fake success until you are successful

- If you want to be a professional trainer, you must embody all the attributes of a professional trainer.

- If you want to be an image consultant, you must look totally fabulous, and behave as if you are totally booked out and influencing the image of lots of satisfied clients.

- People buy perception, people buy energy, and people buy success. They want to be associated with energetic, successful, busy people.

- Your future success depends on projecting present success (no matter how you really feel).

- You hear people saying 'put on your game face'. It's not being a fake person or doing something false.

- It's more about moving to the next level and challenging yourself to live there, even though it may be uncomfortable.

The fake it until you make it rules:

- Have an attitude of success.

- Be firm with yourself, do these three things;

    - Think like a successful you.
    - Look like a successful you.
    - Act like a successful you.

- Always be true to yourself – people see through you if you are not.

- Push yourself out of your comfort zone – it's the only place to grow.

- See the success and act as if you have it – if you don't see it, it won't happen.

- People pick up on energy and see it as an ingredient of success – so project energy.

ꙮ Make your own notes ꙮ

 | 69

Embrace change

Change is one of the most
frightening words in the English
language. It can bring on all
kinds of negative behaviors.

Don't let your reaction to change
be a Pavlovian one. Think it out.
Look behind the obvious.
Change can often be the stimulus
for you to do new things.

Embrace change and use it to
your advantage.

Are you afraid?

Change is one of the most feared notions in people's minds – it's right up there with speaking in public.

Ask yourself how you feel about change. Do you fear it? Do you ignore it? Do you welcome it? Do you actively seek it out and embrace it?

If you fear change, then you could be viewing it as a threat and as something which will make you uncomfortable. It could signal something difficult which might expose your weaknesses and fears.

It's vital to be honest with yourself, so ask yourself why you feel like this. List all your answers and examine them privately. Carry out a reality check on each point. How real are the fears? You will be surprised at what you discover.

It's vital to move to an attitude of welcoming change. I encourage you to actively embrace change. Making change a part of your life forces you to constantly adapt, as you are challenging yourself daily. Personal success involves being adaptable, flexible, and responsive to change.

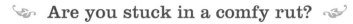 Are you stuck in a comfy rut?

How can you be flexible if you are stuck in a comfy, fur-lined rut? Look at your daily routine and see for yourself just how routine it has become. Start today and change something.

Where do you get your information? Is it from the same source every day? Do you only read the one newspaper, only watch one news program and check one internet site? If so, you are likely to be getting only one perspective. Try to vary your information sources.

For example, if you watch Fox News, start using the internet. Don't believe everything you are told, change the inputs into your brain. The trick is not to only get better but to be different. You need to be open to changing your mind; in doing so, it could change your future.

Am I in a rut?

Have a run through these questions to see if you are in a rut.

- Do I feel totally in my comfort zone?
- When did I last do something that made me uncomfortable?
- Do I seek out challenges or wait for them to find me?
- When did I last look for a new job, assignment, or product?
- Is everything in my life familiar?
- Do I socialise with the same people all the time?

✐ Get out of your rut ✐

Train yourself to look for changes. Always question your comfort level – and do it daily or you run the risk of slowly atrophying.

Go find the first thing to change then do it – today.

First step to get out of a rut

- ✐ Go to work a different way every day.
- ✐ Sit in a different place at meetings.
- ✐ Eat new things.
- ✐ Give up your 'chair' at home.
- ✐ Swap sides of the bed.
- ✐ Read new magazines.
- ✐ Talk to strangers.
- ✐ Talk to your competitors.
- ✐ Talk to members of other political parties.

Always look forward

**Magic happens when you decide to
always look forward.**

**Decide on your Big Audacious Aim (BAA)
and plan everything around achieving it.**

**Once you achieve an aim in your mind
you can then achieve it in reality.**

If you live in the past, you give it huge control over your thinking, resulting in your outlook on life becoming limited by past experiences. Your failures can be given too much attention. Taking your reference from the past can lead to over-analysis.

Do you have this tendency and do you use phrases like:

- If only I had not gone…?
- What if I had done…instead…?
- Perhaps it could have been different if…?
- I always do it this way and look what always happens…?
- This always happens to me…?

❧ Learn from the past and move on ❧

Certainly, one can learn from the past – especially from our mistakes. Mistakes should be seen as an expensive development course – but a course you can't afford to take twice.

That said, however, it's invaluable if you take something away which helps you in the future. But if you stay in the past and wallow in it, you stop moving forward. For this reason, it is extremely good to make looking forward your guiding principle.

Looking forward makes you more action-orientated. You are in control. You decide what to do or what not to do. And remember that every 'non' action is also a decision.

Imagine it's early Monday morning and the week is about to start.

You sit with your coffee and you ask yourself, "What will I do today?"

Why not extend it and ask yourself a bigger question: "What will I do today…this week…this month…this year?" It's that simple – you are in charge of your own destiny.

I know you may want to consider the wishes of your partner, your spouse, your family, and your other responsibilities. But in the end, YOU must be the one who decides.

❧ How to start looking forward ❧

Change the inner chat in your head by using the following key phrases:

- ❧ What can I do today?
- ❧ What will I change today?
- ❧ What will I achieve by Friday?
- ❧ Who would I like to meet and where will I find them?
- ❧ The sky is the limit, so what will I do first?
- ❧ Where would I like to be in five years' time?

❧ Looking forward gives you power ❧

Looking forward allows you to:

- ❧ Escape your past
- ❧ Think big
- ❧ Be proactive
- ❧ Be decisive
- ❧ Be courageous
- ❧ Craft your own destiny
- ❧ Restart
- ❧ Plan long-term
- ❧ Take charge
- ❧ Be bold
- ❧ Do anything

❧ I did this myself ❧

I wanted to spend more time as a professional speaker. I kept saying, "I want to work with large groups of women." I remember sitting at my desk and asking myself, "If I look forward, what are the first five things I need to do?"

This is what I came up with and they guided me for the following year:

1. Write a stunning speech.
2. Practice it with a supportive audience of peers.
3. Redraft it, incorporating feedback, and finalise it.
4. Find willing audiences locally who would like a pro bono speech and deliver it to six audiences.
5. After absorbing the feedback, go out and sell it.

If you had no limitations what would you do?

Look forward one year and say, "I will have…in twelve months' time." Now make a list of five things that you need to do to make it happen.

1. _____

2. _____

3. _____

4. _____

5. _____

Now go do them. Start first thing in the morning.
Don't look back…

Capture your ideas and write them down

When you focus on achieving your Big Audacious Aim, you will be amazed at how ideas come out of the woodwork.

Your mind will start racing and you will have lots of wonderful ideas.

WRITE THEM DOWN. AT ONCE.

It's shocking how we let our best ideas slip away into the cracks in the day. We have wonderful ideas and we think we will remember them. But the reality is that life is too busy and they escape, never to be seen again. What a waste!

⤶ Helpful tips to help capture ⤵ your ideas

1. Have a notebook in your purse, and every time you think of something, jot it down. You will be amazed how fast you will fill it.

2. If you drive a lot, have a recording device with you in your car. You can capture your thoughts as you drive along.

3. Take notebooks on your plane and train journeys. Your body may be trapped in a seat – but your mind is not.

4. Every time you read an article, note down the ideas it sparks in you. Don't just say, "That's a great idea, I must do something." Instead, write it down. When you need inspiration, you will be glad you did.

5. When you are reading fiction, record interesting turns of phrase you encounter. I get fabulous ideas for my speeches from reading good literature from some of the greatest writers in the world.

6. Note striking metaphors you hear. Observe how people use metaphors to explain things to you. When you meet people who work or live in a different world you have discovered a rich source of new metaphors. Think of how differently a city and a rural dweller will make use of metaphors.

7. When you get annoyed by something you read in the newspaper, note your reaction and your thoughts. The odds are that it has also annoyed others – so you've just discovered some food for thought for conversation starters.

8. Listen to feedback and note it. You don't have to take it all on board but if you note it you give yourself the chance to see any patterns. For example, some version of your service may need updating.

9. Look at your initial impressions of new important people in your life as you meet them. This allows you to check back to see if you are good at assessing people or if you miss things.

10. Note down things you suddenly fancy doing – in case you forget. When you need cheering up, this list will be the place to start.

11. When you suddenly think of an absent friend, note their name and what brought them to mind. Contact them and tell them what made you think of them. They will be very touched and you will keep up with your old pals.

12. Note your ideas for writing articles and write a few lines on how you would expand them.

13. Log your observations on a new place. You will learn a lot about your comfort zone, allowing you to know what you may need to challenge yourself on.

14. Keep a travel journal when you go on trips. Your memories get dimmed and you forget the names of people and places.

15. When preparing for a presentation, start well ahead by noting all your thoughts as they occur to you, in no specific order. Stay in the creative flow as that is the hard part. Sorting and editing is always easier once you have the groundwork done.

16. Keep a list of names of books, movies and plays that people mention to you. Then you will always know what to buy in the bookstore or what to go and see.

17. Movies are a wonderful source of ideas. Metaphors like the life journey in the Rocky movies, one-liners such as "Build it and they will come" or "We're going to need a bigger boat".

18. Children have a quirky way of looking at things and can give you a totally fresh perspective. Capture their thoughts for posterity. They will love it in later life.

    My son, when he was little, always mispronounced the word helicopters and called them hepli-chopters. We loved it and can't wait to embarrass him when he is all grown up and sophisticated.

19. Every few weeks, allow yourself the luxury of trawling through your treasure trove of written ideas and see how useful they will be to you as a source of inspiration.

20. Go buy the notebook and cards now.

Record the next ten good ideas you have

1.

2.

3.

4.

5.

6.

7.

8.

9.

10.

 | 81

Donate to the giant favor bank

Live a life of donating to others
from a sense of abundance.
Give of your time and gifts.
Donate to the favor bank by doing
favors for good people.

Other like-minded people are also
donating – so, in time, you will be
repaid a hundredfold.
You just don't know when and
where the repayments will come.

I like to think of life as one giant favor bank. In that bank, there is one
guiding principle or rule: for every favor you do someone, you will be
repaid in kind. You just don't know the person, the place or the time
when this will happen – but it will. Believing this will transform the way
you live.

ᴥ Ask for nothing in return ᴥ

The principle is simple. You do a favor for someone and don't ask for anything in return. Some think that this is crazy and that you will end up as a doormat in no time. They fear they will be thought of as a pushover. In reality it rarely turns out like that – quite the opposite in fact.

Your attitude is crucial. Doing it to curry favor or because you are too weak to say no is not what I mean. I would encourage you to have an attitude of inner strength and self-fulfilment – and then donate from that place in your mind. That is a place of true generosity and power. You are donating because you want to, not because you are obliged to do so.

ᴥ Starting to donate in small ways ᴥ

Start small with gestures like:

ᴥ Driving someone to the airport

ᴥ Cutting your neighbour's grass while they are away

ᴥ Making a meal for a sick friend or neighbor

ᴥ Bringing around a meal when someone has a new baby

ᴥ Offering to baby-sit

They are not a real challenge, but merely a way of limbering up your donating muscles.

A friend in need is a friend indeed

The real donations require you to make concerted effort. My first exposure to this came in my thirties, when I found myself in a management job where I did not fit in with the strong personal agenda of the CEO.

He was making my life extremely unbearable. I was in real difficulty and very unhappy, but could see no way out of it. As often happens in those circumstances, you lose your energy and coping skills just when you need them most. They are drained out of you by the continuous stress.

In the midst of all this, I found myself in a career consultant's office – courtesy of a friend in the recruitment business – for a career coaching session. He was a very kind person and clearly picked up on my distress.

His clear insight allowed him to ask just the right questions to allow me to open up and tell him the whole sorry story. I did not realise how much strain I was under until I started to cry as I told him all about it.

I will never forget how he reacted. He just said: "Right, this is not fair, no one can do this to you, I am going to help you and get you out of there." Straight away I felt better.

He proceeded to help me through negotiations with the company until I was able to leave with excellent references and a financial settlement. He did all of this for free and was incredibly generous with his time and expertise.

Quite literally, he rescued me professionally and taught me quite a few lessons about my self-worth along the way. Ever after, I have always helped people in similar circumstances. If I come across someone being bullied or taken advantage of in a work situation, I offer to help them.

❧ Go to the place of success ❧

I am repaying my debt to the favor bank. Of course, I am also receiving constant paybacks along the way: like the introduction to a potentially good client, the unexpected gift, the timely piece of priceless advice.

Try it out now. Give without expecting a return and see what happens. Help someone when they least expect it – and await the wonderful returns you will receive.

I can honestly say that I have been helped a thousand times over – anything from excellent referrals to wonderful hospitality while traveling or simple kindnesses when I needed them.

❧ Make your own notes ❧

You make your future in your future

Always know where you are going.
Know your destination.

If you don't know where you are going,
you will end up someplace else.

Decide on your future goals and then
live in a way that brings you closer to
them. Don't live in the past – the future
is where opportunity lives.

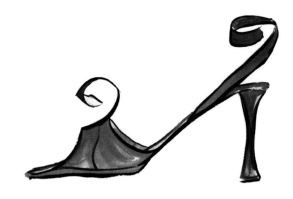

⤙ Successful women have a clearly ⤚ stated vision guiding them

After years of working with truly successful women, I have concluded that a defining characteristic of theirs is that they are future-focussed.

These women are visionaries who feel comfortable with visualising their future and their place in it. They can describe their future state in detail. They can even describe people, places and buildings which will figure in their future, as it is totally real to them.

If you want to really achieve something big, you must adopt that attitude and become a futurist. You must become comfortable with having a future perspective and practice seeing it. Remember Oprah saying early in the presidential campaign that she saw herself at the Inauguration Ball.

The really astonishing ones have a clear and detailed vision, often clearly illustrated on a vision board. They crystallize this future into a clear aim, which is quite awe-inspiring and often a little frightening. The fright gets their adrenaline pumping.

⤙ My Vision ⤚

I found that when I decided on the vision of being an international professional speaker – and used it to guide me – my whole business was transformed. It suddenly allowed a keen focus that set me up for greater levels of success than ever before.

Because I had a firm picture of myself in ten years time, standing on a stage in New York, it pushed me towards working in the United States.

It's up to you. You can stay focused on the present – or you can change. So why not become a futurist and transform your own present?

🌿 Take these 7 steps now to become 🌿 a futurist

Step 1

Take a 10-year perspective on your personal and business life. Whatever your present ideas stretch them out 10 years. And practice being comfortable with more long term thinking.

Step 2

See the essence of your idea not the details. Details bog you down in the present and make you think of problems.

Step 3

Don't be overwhelmed by the practicalities of the next 10 years. Instead, make plans to realize your vision in phases.

Step 4

Realize there will be obstacles, problems, and setbacks. There always are, but see beyond them.

Step 5

Always focus your energy and hope on the end result. It will be your beacon light guiding you. However, it's also sensible to plan for the obstacles!

Step 6

Think big. You are visualizing yourself in 10 years time. Don't make the mistake of having a shorter and easier vision, one that is only two or three years away.

Step 7

Have a positive belief in the 10-year vision. Why not? The 10 years will roll away anyway; why not arrive where you wanted to be rather than some random place?

❧ Go forward a decade. ❧
Make your future in the future

If you want to really be a successful businesswoman, stop living in the present. Successful women have defined their present back from their future. Remember this life-changing concept – go to the future, see it, make your future in your future.

It has a profound effect on women when I ask them to fast-forward to 10 years from now. They suddenly get serious. You do it now. Count out 10 years. Focus on that date. This is the starting point for setting your future.

This is a good exercise because:

- ❧ It removes you from daily hassles.
- ❧ You move beyond the negatives.
- ❧ It opens up your mind to all possibilities.
- ❧ It gives you courage to dream.
- ❧ You take control of your business life.

Don't be merely successful, be significant

Everyone has the chance to leave a legacy before they die. It will be what people remember you for long after you are dead. Rarely do people rate money or a workaholic who never saw their family as a good legacy.

So decide on your legacy. Make a huge difference to this world...be significant.

What does significance mean to you? What do you see as the difference between success and significance? I would like you to think about that for a moment.

Do you ever ask yourself the following questions: "How will I know when I am successful?", "What will success look like?" It's a very grounding experience to figure those answers out.

✍ What is success for you? ✍

Look at some common elements of success and consider if they have relevance in your life. Do you want all of these or just some of them? Which ones are the most important to you?

✍ Money...lots or a reasonable amount

✍ Lovely home

✍ Stylish car

✍ Jewellery

✍ Designer clothes

✍ Designer shoes and handbags

✍ Vacations

✍ Private schools for your children

✍ Ability to buy anything you want without thinking about it

✍ Freedom to do what you want when you want

✍ Work/life balance

✍ Health

✍ Family happiness

✍ Freedom

There are huge benefits to thinking this out and in reminding yourself what you really see as success. Without carrying out this exercise, you could be chasing the wrong things.

✌ Reflect and reassess success ✌

Do you find yourself reassessing and deciding that without health, family and happiness, the rest don't really matter? If so, then look to see how you could translate success into significance.

How would you begin to lead a more significant life? By this, I mean making an impact, being of service and leaving a legacy behind you.

Sometimes it's hard enough for us to define success without stretching it out to significance. So, once you have figured out what you need to do to be successful in your own eyes, to your own standards then it is time to contemplate significance.

Really famous people leave large footprints – but I am not thinking of them. I am thinking of you and me and asking how we could do something that would leave a legacy. Reflect on this. This can be a smaller effort than you think to make a meaningful impact.

✌ Your significance plan ✌

Here are some ideas to get you thinking about it. Remember that when you place being of service to others as a central pivot in your life you really transform your whole life. Giving of your essence is a wonderful gift – especially your time, effort, ideas or energy. Those are things that transform lives.

What would you do?

- Would you use some of your wealth to help transform other's lives?
- Would you give of your expertise – often more valuable than your money?
- How about volunteering your time?
- Would you take a risk and start something new?
- Would you innovate in your work and change how things are done?
- If you see a need in society would you actively work to alleviate it?
- If you see an injustice would you campaign to right it or just leave it to others?

Remember that the power of one is a real force in the world. Everyone is looking for a leader; too few are willing to be that leader. There is a fantastic little poem by an English poet, Roger McGough, which makes you ponder who is in charge and why we are not stepping forward to lead ourselves.

The Leader

I wanna be the leader
I wanna be the leader
Can I be the leader?
Can I? I can?
Promise? Promise?
Yippee I'm the leader
I'm the leader

OK what shall we do?

Roger McGough

Make your message match the messenger

Are you living your message?
Do you look, act and speak in congruence
with who you are?
Do you say you are happy but go around
with a cloud over your head?
Do you advise on health despite being
overweight and a smoker?

People pick up on the
incongruence immediately. So are
you living your message?

When the message matches the messenger, it is called congruence. I remember realising this when I was watching a speaker telling his life story and, at a certain point in the narrative, he had a tear rolling down his cheek. I looked around me to see how this was being received by others as I felt very uncomfortable.

I noticed a similar look of discomfort on many faces. It was coming across as fake. The messenger did not give off the same signals as his story and he came across as incongruent.

The tears were an act. Professional speakers and presenters will tell you that this is a serious challenge for them. Audiences can smell the mixed message from afar.

I find it is no different in any other part of life. People can sense the disconnection.

❧ Entrepreneurs ❧

When I speak to entrepreneurs, I always encourage them to give serious attention to the message they are giving their customers. In my experience, people buy people and then they buy the product or service. Interviewers are very influenced by the personality of the person.

If people are buying you, then they are taking their message from a variety of sources; your appearance, your tone of voice, your body language, your energy, and how all of these connect to what you are selling.

Here are some foolproof tips for making sure you give a congruent message:

- ❧ Always be yourself. People see the real you no matter how you disguise yourself.
- ❧ Always be honest. If you don't know the answer then say so.
- ❧ If it is not right for the client and you know that, say it.
- ❧ Don't pretend to be something you are not.

For example:

If you are in the health or beauty business you really must look and act the part.

If you are in the hospitality business you had better be a people person or you and your customers are both going to be miserable.

Look at your business and make sure you are really representing it well.

❧ The brand consultant ❧

Let me tell you the story of a brand consultant who came to me and said she could help me build my brand. Now if you are building a business on your brand, you will know how protective you are of it. It is a major part of your asset base. You will not let just anybody near it. Like any other potential customer, I am reading the signals she is sending.

If I tell you about the signals you can guess what I decided.

- ❧ She had a good resume.
- ❧ She had good promotional materials.
- ❧ She had a good website.

Yet despite this;

- ❧ She was late.
- ❧ She was very badly presented.
- ❧ She was fumbling and confused.
- ❧ She had poor listening skills.
- ❧ She talked a lot about herself and her careers.
- ❧ She had done no homework.
- ❧ She had done no investigation of my business.

Yes, no surprise that I failed to buy her. The incongruence between her message on her professional materials and her person was too big.

How do you figure out if you, the messenger, match your message?

You do this by thinking like your customer. First of all, who are your customers and what do they expect from you? When you are clear on this, take a very close look at yourself and how you are presenting yourself.

Here is an example:

Judith is a top class designer claiming to be innovative and to customise everything for her customers. Her business was failing and we did a survey of her recent customers to see what was happening in her interactions with them. A glaring finding was the number of comments saying she could not listen.

She could not customise, as she never appeared to take the time to find out what they wanted. So she was indeed innovative – but it was **her** innovation, **her** ideas, from **her** mind. She was seen to be foisting her innovation onto her customers. While they might use her once, they would never give her repeat business.

The **messenger** thought the message was: I listen and design innovative concepts that match your needs.

The **message** was: I know what is best and my talent will come up with the solution.

Have a very good look at who you are dealing with on a daily basis and then have an equally good look at yourself (the messenger) and your message. If in doubt, ask people who will give you constructive feedback, but beware of asking any psychic vampires.

Explore other domains

Most of us live in a limited number
of domains.
We are technology people, artistic
people, communication people,
information people, engineers,
bankers, scientists, or family people.
We get imprisoned in one.
We speak a jargon peculiar to us and
our closest friends and colleagues.

To stimulate your mind, it is good
to escape and explore a completely
different domain.

A domain is a particular area or sector. Good examples are IT, medicine, publishing, speaking, or painting. Domain knowledge is the knowledge you gain in a particular field – like a school or university – or a particular subject like any of the ones listed above.

People can live or work in a particular domain and get confined in it. People in one domain share a deep understanding of a confined area; they speak in a domain-specific language.

Have you ever sat with two techies and felt you were visiting from another planet and yet to learn the language? Medical people do the same; all the conditions have names with initials or Latin names known only to those in the field.

⟨ Master something different ⟩

The key question is whether you live primarily in one domain. Did you study in a specialized area and are you now working in the same area? Examples of this are accountancy, banking, IT, education, law, medicine, and health care. You get the point.

I remember spending the early part of my career in the domain of Third World development. I would happily sit with my fellow citizens of this cozy world and talk of ODA (Overseas Development Assistance) NICS (Newly Industrializing Countries), UNDP, UNESCO, UNICEF and a myriad of other UN (United Nations) bodies. We never realized that we were talking complete rubbish to an outsider.

My challenge to you is to actively go outside your domain on a daily basis and explore at least two other domains. Peter Drucker, the management guru, recommended that you master at least two domains in your life.

⟨ The payback ⟩

When you fill your brain with information from very divergent places, you are literally forcing it to work with new concepts and new information. The payback for this comes when you have to solve complex problems with no immediate solution. Most personnel problems fall into this category.

Payback 1: Thinking of the problem from all sides

How you solve a problem depends on how you think of it. Your thinking will depend on the mental representation you make of the problem in the first place. The more divergent your sources of information and the more information you have at your fingertips, the greater your chances of solving the problem.

Payback 2: Insightful thinking

When you see the problem, you represent it in a certain way in your head – this depends on many factors: your knowledge, your beliefs, your experiences. Insightful thinking involves breaking free of an inappropriate representation that prevents us from seeing the problem clearly.

Payback 3: Transfer of ideas

This means applying knowledge learned in one situation to a new situation. However, people don't often transfer this information. This is because they don't dig deep enough to find the generic similarities. The more you do this, the more creative your brain becomes.

✎ Make a simple start in changing ✎ self-limiting beliefs

Stop all your self-limiting behaviors that keep you trapped in a particular area. Classic examples include:

I don't like reading fiction. I am more comfortable with facts.

Go get a classic novel like Huckleberry Finn or a Charles Dickens novel – and read it. For one thing, it will immediately increase your vocabulary.

I only like escapist literature.

Read the business section of your local paper every day.

I would never read a current affairs magazine. It's all too depressing.

Go buy Time, Newsweek, or Forbes.

I never visit art galleries. That's not for me.

Go to your local art gallery or art exhibition. Feed your visual brain, it is very important to progress your thinking skills.

I hate sport. I would never go to a game.

Sport played well can be poetry in motion.

I have never been to a library.

They are free and a treasure trove of unbelievable knowledge.

I would rather eat pins than read the Financial Times.

Start with your local business papers. Remember the Financial Times is pink!

I know nothing about nature.

You are missing out on a whole new way of understanding the world.

✎ Start tomorrow ✎

What other domain would you like to explore? Where would you like to start? What one thing will you do tomorrow to get started?

✎ Make your own notes ✎

Act strategically to achieve your Big Audacious Aim

To make your dream happen, you must have a strategic plan. If you are serious about realising your BAA, you must adopt a goal-focussed approach to life.

Set your priorities and then set out the clear steps to reach each stage in your plan. You will not succeed if you approach it in a haphazard fashion, with no ideas of targets and time frames.

How do I plan strategically?

Forget jargon! Planning jargon gets in the way of clear thinking. Just use one set of words and stick to them. One word is as good as another – so use mine for this exercise and you can develop your own over time.

Here are some fundamentals to strategic planning:

- A strategic plan should be crystal clear and concise, not a telephone book.
- Forget all the planning jargon; aims, objectives, goals, visions, actions. The best plans use simple English. If you don't understand the words you won't action it.
- Short is best in plans. Long-winded plans end up on shelves.
- You must write it yourself. You won't own it if an advisor writes it.
- It must be anchored in common sense.
- If you have run a home, brought up children, you are a strategic planner.
- Lots of experts in strategic planning build a mystique around it. Don't believe them.

The basis of a good strategic plan is good strategic thinking. If you think strategically, you can write a good strategic plan – given the right tools.

Five Strategic Thinking Pointers

- Start in the future and look back. Never start in the present and work forward.
- Focus on the end result.
- Always clarify the major components first. Don't go into details too soon.
- Think of the whole thing as a triangle. The main aim at the pinnacle, the goals in the next layer down and the actions at the bottom of the triangle. It must fit together logically with one aim on top, up to seven goals next and up to ten specific actions under each goal.
- Think of your plan as a cascade of a waterfall. See it in its entirety and then cascade down through the layers.

Don't try to do everything. Set your Big Audacious Aim.

This will be the most strategic decision you make. I think that deciding what not to do is more difficult than deciding what to do.

I have seen women really struggle with setting a BAA because they can't let things go. They want to have a lot of aims and can't focus on one. Sadly, they end up doing all of them poorly.

I sympathize with this dilemma as I see it all the time in my SHOES programs – but I can guarantee you that when women focus and plan, they are truly deadly. All that creativity and talent is focused in a laser-like ray of energy.

✒ My Big Audacious Aim ✒

A number of years ago, I was deciding to change careers and found myself on the horns of this dilemma. I had worked for many years in the leadership of the not-for-profit world and had set up a successful consultancy, working worldwide with international organizations on leadership.

However, I had had enough. I was no longer getting a thrill from the work. So I decided to focus on my passion in life, which was helping women to be hugely successful and to get to the top.

I spent one whole year between the two ideas; consultant to the not-for-profit sector, working with women along the way or setting up a whole new venture focusing exclusively on women.

I was like someone with one foot on the shore and the other on the boat. Not a comfortable place to be. Finally, I was making a presentation to a group of business colleagues in a business network on new directions in my work. I stood up and made an off-the-cuff presentation about what I would really like to do.

I described the SHOES program, which was in the conceptual stage (an idea in my head) and found myself getting very passionate and emotional.

When I sat down, the Chairperson asked what had happened to Veronica. "Who is this person, all lit up, full of energy and drive? Where is the other consultant gone?" That decided me. I started work on the Big Audacious Aim the next day and the whole SHOES brand began.

What was fantastic was the way everything changed when I made a decision and became strategic. The way new opportunities came my way was astonishing. I started behaving more strategically when I had drawn up a strategic plan to deliver my BAA.

Don't be a hoarder, let things go

Too many possessions clutter your life.
Start decluttering with your wardrobe.
You only wear 20% of what you own.
Let go of all the things you don't wear.

Do the same with your other
possessions. Let things go when they
have served their purpose. What can
you let go of now?

Hoarders come in all shapes and sizes. They hoard all manner of surprising things, from actual physical clutter to remnants from their deep past, or emotions, grudges and psychic wounds from long ago.

If you hoard things, you clutter up not just your physical space, but also the thinking space in your mind.

✌ Hoarding possessions ✌

I had a wake-up call recently when I worked with a group of image consultants. These are the wonderful people who help you look your best – no matter what size or shape you may be. I can tell you it was one of the biggest challenges of my life getting dressed that morning!

They gave me the important news that 80% of my closet never saw the light of day and that 20% never got into the closet as it was always on my back. I couldn't believe it. How could these women know me so well when they had never been in my bedroom? They even offer a de-cluttering service – imagine that!

Are you like me? Do you have an amazing purple dress that fitted ten years ago and was so expensive it's never going to be dumped – even though it wouldn't even fit over my arm right now? Are you hoarding like this?

Get rid of all the old stuff now. How can you look smart and up to the minute if you can't even get one new item into the closet?

Hoarding stifles you

A client of mine is in the training and consultancy business and she came to me saying she had lost her energy and her business was stalled. She asked me could I help her get her mojo back so she could recover and re-launch her business.

I went around to her offices and do you know what I found? An Aladdin's cave! She had client files from the 1980s, reports as far back as 1990. Her office was pointed firmly towards the past.

Worse was out the back where we found training materials from the medieval ages – acetates and black-and-white handouts curling at the edges. Her materials were older than some of her trainees. She even had back copies of her out of date books, all piled up.

If a new idea had come in the door, it would have died from lack of air. Her problem was abundantly clear. Her space, her office, her life – and even her mind – were totally cluttered from decades of hoarding so many things.

The first thing she did was perform a massive clean out. It took her four days. She was ruthless. It was a cathartic experience. She told me it was the best experience she had for years.

It caused her to re-evaluate her whole approach as if she was stuck in the past. It was no wonder clients had gone elsewhere in search of more up-to-date answers. She made a huge new space for all the new ideas and new clients to pour in. Her business recovered and now she has an annual clearout.

ᔌ What are you hoarding? ᔍ

Have a look around you. Are you hoarding things in your home or your business? Why are you doing this? Is it that you haven't noticed it accumulating – or is there a deeper reason? Think about it, but not for long. Get out the black plastic bags and go for it.

ᔌ Hoarding the past ᔍ

People get stuck in the past because they are terrified of the present, not to mention the future. Surprisingly, all kinds of people become stuck. Some seemingly successful people could be twice as successful, but are held back by having one foot in the past and one foot in the present.

It always amazes me that people cannot let go of their experiences of the past. They seem to provide nourishment and comfort. Many wounded people stay cowering in the past. The wound is too deep for them to move beyond it, so they stay there nursing it.

It is very sad to watch, and to feel powerless to do anything. They need to decide themselves to let it go and to move on. I have a friend whose husband left her many years ago and she still gives a lot of her energy to that man and that period in her life. It is difficult for her to let it go.

Find the reason you can't move from the past. Expose it to the light of day and it will begin to lose its power over you. You can't have one foot on the shore and one foot on the boat...let one go.

Have courage. Have a look around and begin the de-cluttering at once. You have only your junk to lose.

Find the best and benchmark against them

Benchmark against the best.

Find the best person or company in your field. Study them.

Find out the ingredients of their excellence and their success. That is the standard you set for yourself – the best. Emulate it.

You can't go wrong when you start at excellence and work from there.

Learn from the best

Learning from the best is an enormous boost to any person or company. Learning companies will go anywhere to find the best teachers. A good place to start is by looking at your own suppliers and customers. Are any of them renowned for excellent service?

Why? Talk to them about their service. You will be surprised how helpful they can be. This approach can be used to improve overall service in your company or to overcome a specific difficulty.

If you discover that you are having difficulty with one aspect of the business (such as telephone sales) find out who runs the most efficient telephone sales operation and approach them. They may not operate in your sector, but they will have solved problems similar to yours.

❧ The Learning Curve ❧

1. Identify the area you want to improve.

2. Find out who is excellent in this area. Look at customers, suppliers, competitors or companies in any sector.

3. Involve your staff in the search for examples of "excellence," especially the staff performing the functions requiring improvement.

4. Approach the other company. Offer to share solutions to mutual problems.

5. Arrange to visit them.

6. Prepare carefully in advance. The group who visit should be clear about their questions and what their problems are. However, they should also have an open mind about all aspects of the business.

7. Meet and discuss experiences at once, preferably before returning to work. Decide what changes, if any, are needed.

8. Designate someone to see that changes are enacted and to act as coach/minder to those carrying out changes.

❧ Benchmarking ❧

You can also use this approach to set standards for the overall organization. Many companies seek out the best competitor then set their standards at this level and seek to better it. This form of benchmarking can have a powerful effect on your company and staff. It is challenging.

❧ How to benchmark ❧

You look at the best, compare it to what you do and aim to close the gap. Quite often, the difference is in attitudes, in actions of the staff, in the company culture or management style. Bridging the gap may not necessarily mean spending vast amounts of money, it could mean changing attitudes; something which is often slower and more difficult than spending money.

By all means, start with companies similar to your own – but also be imaginative. Think laterally. If you run a bus tour company, serving elite, top-class clients, then look at other service providers serving the same type of client.

You could check out top-class hotels or boat hire companies. What you have in common is your type of customer: elite, top-class, hard to please and with exacting standards.

Send your staff out to experience the best

If you run a hotel, send staff to stay in other hotels. Work out a questionnaire with them in advance. Sit down and spend time analyzing it on their return. It's not a holiday, it's a work assignment.

If you run any form of eatery, send your staff out to others. Pick the best. Watch everything they do: from the initial greeting, level of attention to customers, number of errors, decor, uniforms, and cleanliness. If you are in the retail sector visit the best and most expensive shops. What is it about them that makes them special? Can you adopt any of their innovations?

❧ Benchmarking ❧

- ❧ Find others with excellent practices and set your standard at their level. Check regularly to see if your standards are better, the same, or slipping. You can do this for every aspect of your business.

- ❧ Set benchmarks of best practice and set up systems to ensure they are met. This also defines what is unacceptable and lets everyone know what is expected.

- ❧ Keep looking for examples of excellence in your industry or sector. Be aware of the benchmarks for your industry – the industry norm.

❧ You can also learn from the worst ❧

You can also learn from bad experiences. When examining other companies, you will come across some badly run outfits. You'll find all sorts of businesses where the customers are treated as if they don't matter. Watch these companies closely – for as long as they exist.

Identify the top three reasons why you feel the company is failing its customers. Examine your company and see if those three failures apply to your company – and discover if you may have cause for concern.

Nordstroms is extremely famous for its customer service. So famous that people speak about "Nordstroming" their service. Betsy Sanders once wrote a book about the "Nordstrom Way" entitled Fabled Service Ordinary Acts, Extraordinary Outcomes. In it, she says: "Fabulous service is quite simply ordinary people doing ordinary things, extraordinarily well."

We could all practice that.

Find your adult state

Inside each of us are three states:
adult, parent and child.

You are in one state at any one time.
Your challenge is to stay in the adult state.
The most productive interactions take place
when both people are in the adult state.

Do not go into the parent or child state,
even when you are provoked.

I am a great believer in having everyone behave as rationally as possible, especially in a business setting. However, over the years of working at all levels of organizations I realise this is not a given.

There are a lot of grown up children out there in the workplace. Sometimes you have to be careful or if you don't duck, like a recent president, you will get hit in the head – but not by a shoe, by their toys.

Are we letting 'children' run our businesses?

I find a certain type of man in business who, when crossed, climbs into his pram and if he does not get his own way, he throws all his toys right at you. Have you come across this person?

There is way too much childish behavior in business and lack of emotional control. I read recently about the levels of testosterone in Wall Street, causing young traders to become greater risk takers. When things started to go bad, the hormone levels went down – making them highly risk adverse. Could this be a case of raging teenage hormones?

❧ Transactional analysis ❧

I came across a very clear-cut and simple way of dealing with this outbreak of childlike behavior – it's called transactional analysis.

Transactional analysis puts forward the viewpoint that every event that happens to you is etched on your brain in some way. It says that things that happen to you can cause this event to be recalled, causing you to react instantly.

Think of how certain smells trigger memories. When you hear a particular song, you are catapulted back to a beach in your youth. You know how this happens. Some are lovely, others are not. Some can be downright painful.

There are three different states of mind: **adult, child and parent.**

You can only be in one state at any one time. The events described above can trigger you to go into any one of these states. The behavior of the person with you can also be a trigger.

Here is the challenge: the best interactions take place between two adults, so that is where you want to be and where you want to place the other person. The danger comes when:

❧ Either of you goes into the parent state, as that pushes the other into the child state.

❧ Either of you goes into child state, as that pushes the other into the parent state.

❧ Children and parents in the office ❧

These are the situations you want to avoid:

❧ You go into an office to have a word with a direct report about something that needs improvement. If you say anything that sounds like a mummy comment, they see you as being in parent state and you can get a childish response.

This is not good for the professionalism of the office and very hard to recover from. So avoid the corrective "I know better", "buck up" kind of parent comments.

❧ Someone comes into your office with a request and you are not pleased to see them, so you become difficult, do a bit of whinging and complaining about the unfairness of being asked to do this.

You act like a kid and the person goes into your worst version of your mother and tells you to get over yourself and do it by 5pm that day – or else. This is a typical authoritarian parent move.

❧ Make your own notes ❧

| |
| |
| |
| |
| |

Are there 'children' in your business?

Have a think. Are there situations in your life where you think you are surrounded by a bunch of kids, not your own, but the rest of the adults in your life? If so, then start using this approach. Remember, adult-to-adult is what you desire.

How do you get people into adult state?

Use phrases like:

Can we agree on an approach to this problem?

I know you are upset, but we must find a solution to this problem.

I completely understand how you feel but, nonetheless, we must solve this issue.

Always show you understand their position but also that the two of you need to get on with business.

The bottom line is that both parties need to stay in the adult state if you're to make progress – so leave the kiddishness to the kids.

Thrive not survive

Are you thriving or surviving?

Life is too short to simply survive.
What does thriving look like? List the top 5
things that would allow you to thrive.
Now make a plan to get them. Surprise yourself.
Always aim to thrive.

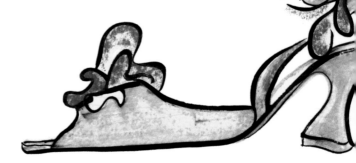

❧ You don't need money to thrive ☙ and be happy

Every day at every moment, we make the decision to either survive or thrive – this starts in our heads. For a number of years, I worked visiting development projects in very poor countries in Africa and Asia, where you would expect to find terrible unhappiness. Yet despite the appalling financial circumstances, I often found great dignity and a sense of contentment.

I found this particularly true in Africa, where people were often happy with small things. They lived each moment of each day. I learnt a lot from these experiences: happiness is not about possessions, it's much more to do with your state of mind, your contentment with your life, and your sense of place in the world.

ꙮ It's more than fame ꙮ

Happiness is such an ephemeral thing that it eludes many. It is so sad to see people of wealth and fame complaining about not being happy.

So often, they just need to stop, to readjust their perceptions and their thinking. Don't you just want to tell the celebrities you see moaning on TV to get a life?

ꙮ Choose your path ꙮ

Everyone travels a path in life, whether consciously or unconsciously. For many of us, it's an unconscious path, made up of routine and humdrum events. We can get into the trap of working to eat, to go on holidays and then go back to work to eat and save for the next holiday. This is a hard path to be on. Yet many people live like this: they are merely surviving.

If this is you, now is the time to be courageous and ask yourself if you are surviving or thriving. If you think you are merely surviving then you are not yet on your true 'path.' You need to rethink. Being on your path should have a sense of rightness and excitement about it. It should feel like you are living fully – thriving instead of surviving.

❧ Thrive with your children ❧

You can get in touch with your life's path when you begin to figure out what living a thriving life would look like. Would it mean working harder? Hardly. More likely it means spending more time with family and friends.

I often wonder at people who spend their children's entire childhood on the road and then can't understand why their teenagers have no relationship with them. Their chance at parenthood passed them by and they discovered this too late. It's good to realize that you only get a loan of your children for a short number of years.

❧ Make your own notes ❧

✎ Thriving in business is the only way ✎

There is a real danger in the current economic climate of adopting a survival attitude to your business. It's as if we have all drawn up the drawbridges and gone into our strongholds to hibernate. This is not the way to have your business thrive.

This is the time when you work harder at customer satisfaction and seeing everything through their eyes. They can be much more choosey now and they will not choose a business which has cut its level of service. Now is not the time to compete on price and join the race to the bottom.

Now is the time to compete on service and to really work on wowing each and every person who interacts with your business. This level of action is fueled by energy and positivity. Scrimping and saving and being miserable will not save your business. Going into baseline survival mode will kill your spirit – and your business.

Why survive when you could thrive?

Fall

When I was in school, studying literature by Irish writers, we all learnt the poems of William Butler Yeats and my favorite one was The Wild Swans At Coole. When I was writing the autumn or fall Shoeisms, I was picturing his 59 beautiful swans sitting in magnificent tranquility on the beautiful lake in Co Sligo, in Ireland.

These are the exact lines from the poem.

"The trees are in their autumn beauty,
The woodland paths are dry,
Under the October twilight the water
Mirrors a still sky;
Upon the brimming water among the stones
Are nine-and-fifty Swans."

These Fall Shoeisms are a blueprint for a woman's survival today.

❧ Helpful tips to help capture ❧ your ideas

There are times in our life when we need to take a break from the creative generation of new ideas and the bountiful living of life to the full, and go quiet and calm. These Shoeisms are to help you when you need to go into that space.

Fall is when nature slows down and conserves energy. The fall Shoeisms will help you to prioritize ways of conserving your essence and avoid wasting your energy and emotions.

Women are the last great multitaskers, always trying to do too many things at once. The pressures on women today are really very serious and potentially detrimental to mental and physical health. More women than ever are in the workforce, are working longer hours, are the principal caregivers to their children and also to their elders. And as always, women do more of the housework.

We concentrate a lot on how to stay positive and upbeat, but I also think we need to take a step back and look at the very foundations we are building for that positivity. Without good foundations, we cannot build a sustainable, positive attitude.

I am thinking of the serenity of swans against the background of rich, mellow, yellowing leaves and the rich smell of ripening berries and apples. I strongly believe each of us has to spend some time in that fall, enjoying the natural slow pace of fading summer and the richness of approaching autumn.

To be ready to survive the current hard realities, we must spend some of our time in fall mode, slowing down, conserving our energy and adopting strategies that will conserve our essence for the right things. We must learn to stop wasting our energy on monkey people, our dominating inner 'big sis', on negative people, on useless questions or on regrets. Instead, we need to build a bubble around our essential selves, build our self-belief, and conserve our energy – all within our own healthy boundaries.

Detach the monkey people

Life is hard enough without going through it with a swarm of monkey people attached to your back. Meet this new type of person in this Shoeism so you can detach them and cut off their draining power.

Build a positive energy bubble around you

It's not possible to donate energy and sunshine to the universe and accept all the trials of life without losing some of your inner strength. Use your own personal bubble.

With self-belief you can do anything

The power of self-belief is unbelievable, but until you realize this and tap into it, you may be operating at less than your true strength. Incorporate this into your life.

Tell 'big sis' where to get off

Have you had a chat with your 'big sis' recently? Do you even realize she is there and are you aware of her power to destroy your inner resolve? Use this Shoeism to meet her and find out how to put her in her place.

Make your body your temple

Many women forget that their health is their wealth and don't make their body their temple. Are you like that? Do you forget yourself and get run down? See if any of these temple-building tips can work for you.

Don't waste your anger

Anger is a powerful emotion and can be used to great effect if channeled properly. Do you use your anger like that? Check and see how big a part it is in your life – and how you use it.

Don't harbor resentments

Unresolved anger coalesces into resentment, and if you carry it around for any length of time, it has the same effect as acid. Take a reality check and see if you can preserve your peace by dropping any resentment.

Withdraw from negativity

In the mellow space associated with fall, I would like you to draw back from the energy sapping effect of negativity.

Surround yourself with enriching people

Have a look at the people all around you in your life and assess whether they are a negative or positive force in your life. Distance your self from the negatives and embrace the positives.

Don't answer questions, respond to them

Are you falling into the trap of answering other people's endless questions? Look at this and see how to stop that exhausting activity. Conserve your energy for your priorities.

Beware resistance

Are you as surprised as I am at how the oddest forms of resistance surface just as you decide to take a big decision? Comfort yourself that you are not alone by reading and adopting this Shoeism to help you with your next big decision.

Be realistic with yourself

Why are we so unrealistic with ourselves? We set too high goals and are then hard on ourselves. Stop that. Use this advice to forgive yourself and lower the bar.

Life is too short for regrets

This should be given out on signs in the supermarket. Release yourself from a lot of grief by exploring this one, and seeing if you can adopt it as a life maxim.

Have clear boundaries

The foundation of all inner calm is knowing where you begin and others end. This is a hard one for women because of their nurturing role, but you stand to lose too much if you have vague boundaries. Check your boundaries out here.

Detach the monkey people

If you feel you are being asked to do too much, you may have 'monkey people' in your life. Imagine, at your next meeting, that some people have little monkeys sitting on their shoulders. Each request for you to do something is a monkey. Their aim is to transfer as many monkeys as possible to your shoulders.

Don't accept them. Make sure they leave with all their monkeys!

The term 'monkey people' comes from all my years of working with senior and middle managers, helping them to improve their performance. I coined it to describe the people who always try to dump their problems onto you.

It will come as no surprise to you when I say that most managers' problems can be traced to people and their concerns. I found that a lot of managers had difficulty with issues like delegating, setting boundaries, following through, making people responsible, and accountability: all issues that were interrelated at some level. Key components were often the inexperience or lack of skills of the manager and the way they failed to deal with monkey people.

⊱ When Monkeys Rule ⊰

This is one of my favorite stories – it's about Janice, a woman I worked with who was the manager of a medium-sized firm in the service sector. We had begun working together and she was sitting across from me in a very distressed state as she revealed her story. She felt completely overwhelmed by the behavior of her staff.

She gave them things to do but never followed up, so they quickly established that she had no system of recalling delegated jobs, and they took complete advantage of her inefficiency. She was very casual with some members of staff and formal with others, leading to confusion. Even though she had delegated tasks, she went ahead and did them herself if she found them undone at the end of the week.

She assumed all real responsibility, never passing it down the line. In truth, she considered her staff 'irresponsible' and made them unaccountable, so the staff began working at the lowest possible level, that of specific tasks or actions.

They learnt from her that she liked control and did not trust them, so they adopted two strategies for survival: they came to her with every little item they were unsure of and completely hid the rest from her until there was a crisis, whereupon they dumped it on her desk and ran. No wonder she was distressed. She was a classic creator and nourisher of monkey people.

I asked her to give me actual examples of what happened on a daily basis, detailing every aspect of her behavior when someone came into her office. A series of repeating stories revealed a pattern. She was letting her staff get away with murder. They were passing on all their difficult or unpleasant tasks to her. They were asking for permission for minor things. They were failing to take any responsibility – and she was aiding and abetting them. As she told me more and more stories, she began to see the underlying pattern begin to emerge.

Pass the monkey

Her staff were coming in saying things like:

- I can't find the keys *(meaning "Can you get them for me?")*
- I can't order the supplies until you look at the catalogue *(meaning "I want you to order as you won't like what I do.")*
- I can't book the serviceman until you read the specifications *(meaning "I want you to take charge.")*
- I can't write the report until you tell me the headings *(meaning "You don't trust me, so I'm going to wait until you spoonfeed me.")*

Do you get the picture? By her own behaviors, she was creating a whole tribe of monkey people.

She continued telling me the stories and after every one I placed a toy monkey on her shoulder (I am lucky as my family was caught up with the beanie baby craze a few years ago, so we have lot of beanie baby monkeys.) With each story came a new monkey, and very quickly she was covered in them – they were crawling all along the armrest of her chair onto the table.

Boy, did she get the point! I explained that every one of those monkeys belonged to someone else. They were not hers. Her job was to change the way she behaved and to delegate with responsibility and accountability. So every time a monkey person came in carrying a monkey, she was to view it suspiciously and make sure the person left with their monkey.

ᔓ Detach the monkeys ᔒ

She was to envisage the monkey getting off the person and coming to her desk and to watch for the key monkey phrases:

ᔓ Only you have the expertise to do this, so I am leaving it to you.

ᔓ I don't feel equipped to do this.

ᔓ I will not have it done in time, so can you do it for me?

ᔓ I have too much to do, I need you to help.

They are monkey transferring phrases. I told her she had to watch for these and then to change her behavior – to change them to empowering phrases such as:

ᔓ I trust you to do this.

ᔓ I will show you how to do this now so next time you will know how to do it on your own.

ᔓ Have another look at the problem and come back to me with a couple of your suggestions to fit it – I will be happy to discuss them with you.

Janice was transformed. She realised that she had created her own monsters by her management style and only **she** could change it. The monkey people metaphor allowed her to see the problem.

ᔓ Apply this to yourself ᔒ

Look around you. Think about your behaviors. These monkeys exist everywhere; in work, in partners, in spouses, in teenagers (especially in teenagers), in children, and in hapless friends.

They are easy to recognize as they all share the common characteristic of someone wanting you to do something that they should be doing themselves. They are coaxing, manipulating, guilting, or asking you to take charge of it. They play on your busyness, inattention; need to help, need to be liked or some such emotion. Are you growing monkey people?

Don't get suckered. Take no monkeys – free or otherwise. Begin detaching them now.

Build a positive energy bubble around you

To protect your positive energy, you must create a positive bubble of energy in a 360 degree circle around you.

Every morning in the shower, imagine a giant bubble around you – it's your positive space so fill it with all your positive thoughts and energies. Then zip it up tight.

As you go through your day, you are subject to wear and tear – emotionally, mentally and physically. So it makes sense to protect yourself in advance. I recommend that you start every day by surrounding yourself with a big fat energy bubble. I suggest that you put it on in the shower or immediately after your shower.

How to make your energy bubble

- Stand upright and imagine that you have grown a third leg coming out of your spine and going into the ground to a distance of two feet.
- Extend your bubble into the ground to that depth.
- Now put your arms out in front of you as far as they will go and push the bubble out to that distance.
- Put your hands up in the air as high as they will go and that is the top of the bubble.

You have created a bubble which goes two feet under you, two feet all around you and two feet into the air. This is your protective bubble which surrounds you for the rest of the day.

The next stage is to fill it with positive energy. To do this, you need to think of something very positive and very exhilarating that has happened to you in the past. See it and feel it.

Feel the energy associated with it and pour that into your bubble. When it's full, seal it up. This means that you are set for the day. Do it every morning, but especially on days you expect to be difficult or draining for you.

Protect your energy bubble

Don't allow any energy drainers into that private space. I remember doing this when my son was very small and he was so delighted with the concept that he insisted on making his own energy bubble.

We had great fun when we decided that we could unzip our bubbles and join them up to make one big bubble for the two of us. I think it introduced him to the concept of protecting his own energy.

When you are with real energy drainers, it can put you under tremendous strain and you need to realise that they are trying to drain you. You need to know that your bubble will protect you.

The highest energy always wins

It is good to know that in any interaction the person with the highest energy wins. Any trainer who prepares people for an interview will tell the candidate to hype up their energy as part of their preparations. The interview panel must feel their energy when they enter the room. It sets the tone for the whole interaction.

Having high energy and having it protected is very useful in all kinds of situations where your energy may be taken from you:

- Negotiations
- Conflict resolution
- Interviews
- Presentations

⋙ Prepare for meetings with ⋘ energy drainers

Always beware of energy drainers. I always put a big bubble in place when I know I am meeting people who have the potential to drain my energy.

I used this to great effect when I was working in Bosnia Herzegovina, in a mediation role between people of very differing viewpoints. There was always the possibility they would view me as the common outsider and unite against me.

There was a serious amount of unresolved conflict from the civil war simmering just under the surface, and people could be destructively negative. I realised after my first trip that my energy bubble was a vital part of my toolkit.

I introduced all the wonderful people I worked with to the whole idea. They laughed at first at this woman from Ireland with her bubble. However, when they saw how it worked in a number of difficult situations, I converted them. They were impressed that I could survive very difficult interactions and still seem to have energy and good cheer.

A happy development was when I came back for another assignment and the team met me at the airport and told me they had evolved my bubble routine. They decided that they were going to choose a different membrane depending on the day.

So on really bad days, with lots of potentially difficult and hostile interactions, they were going to have a titanium membrane. Steel was a lesser option for less difficult situations, but hard metals were their choice.

I was thrilled that they had adopted it so thoroughly and made it their own. So when you need cheering up, think of all the metal bubbles moving around the Balkans!

Create your energy bubble tomorrow morning!

With self belief, you can do anything

Self belief is a core element of success. Your best reserves are within your own head.

Look inside and see the possibilities. Build your self belief by always noting and celebrating your successes.

What do you think is the number one issue for women in business today? I am fascinated by this search. Think about it for a moment. I always ask groups of women what their number one issue is and I have found that self belief is the one mentioned the most. It also comes up as the main thing holding women back on all of my SHOES programs.

❧ How does lack of self belief show up? ❧

I believe that self belief is a core element of success. You must have total belief in yourself if you are going to be really successful in business today. I don't mean outward confident behavior, I mean that inner self belief which defines you and what you think you can achieve.

Look at these scenarios and see if any of them resonate with you.

1. Do you hesitate in starting a business even when you have a great idea?
2. Do you hesitate to ask for a salary increase or a bonus when you know you deserve it?
3. Do you get the right amount of credit for what you achieve?
4. Are you charging enough for your services?
5. Are you thinking big enough?
6. Do you allow negative people to discourage you?

If they do, then you may need to spring clean your self belief system with three fundamental steps:

Take a good positive look at yourself

Realistically, examine yourself from a business perspective and see the things you are good at. We do not do this enough. List your qualifications, experience, successes and attributes. Do it honestly but positively. If you don't celebrate your own strengths, who else will?

See what others find unique about you

Ask positive supportive colleagues to tell you one thing which makes you unique in what you do. This is a wonderful way to discover, in a positive way, what others think of you. When you've done so, know and celebrate your successes.

Take time to write down successes of the last year

Crucial to self belief is realising how good you are, believing it, recording your successes and, finally, savoring and celebrating them.

Gather all this information while being realistic with yourself. Realise how good you are. I find women become angry when they see others getting the jobs they wanted or setting up the business they wanted.

I tell them that the only difference between those who do and those who don't is that one set went out and did it – and one didn't. Why? They believed they could – and they did. Meanwhile, you hesitated and postponed and let the opportunity slip.

You know, once you become determined to stand up and be something amazing, the most wonderful things happen to help you. So it is crucial that you claim your space. To help you do this, I have put together a set of principles to guide you in building your powerful self belief.

✎ Make your own notes ✎

✍ Ten and a half principles to build ✍ a powerful self belief

✍ Five must dos ✍

- ✍ Do something frightening every day because everything you ever wanted is on the other side of fear.
- ✍ Find what you are excellent at, stick to it and build a fantastic reputation.
- ✍ Invest in yourself. Commit to life long learning – because you are worth it.
- ✍ Let things go. You need to make space for new opportunities.
- ✍ Keep upping your value.

✍ Five must not dos ✍

- ✍ Do not mistake money for power. Claim the power and the money follows.
- ✍ Concentrate on building relationships with your customers.
- ✍ Don't dishonor yourself by doing work beneath your level of expertise.
- ✍ You can't afford the luxury of one negative thought.
- ✍ You must not harbor regrets – life is way too short.

✍ And a half ✍

- ✍ Do not get out of bed for less than your daily value. Ever!

Tell 'big sis' where to get off

All of us have a big sister sitting
on our shoulder commenting on
our aspirations and actions.
It is our inner critic telling us
how we fail, what we do wrong or
how we could do better.

Tell her to shove off. You don't
need her. Be wary as she will
not go easily. You will need to be
persistent to firmly dislodge her.

All of us have a big sister sitting on our shoulder, ready to give a comment on everything we think and do. This is our inner critic who is our constant companion through life. Some of us are cursed with a very vocal critic and so we feel we need to second guess everything.

'Big sis' comes in many different forms and it is good to know the signs of her presence so that you can isolate and silence her. Not everyone has these ladies on their shoulders all the time, but have a look and ask if one of them seems familiar to you.

❧ The 'you are not good enough' sis ❧

This is where she feeds into your deep-seated fear that you are not quite good enough at anything you do. She drives you to perfection where you don't make any mistakes and have complete control over your organised world. Your big sis gets disappointed with you or others when the high expectations are not met

This big sis needs to be quietened down and the pressure to be perfect removed if she is to be controlled. You know that it is not possible to control the world completely, so why drain yourself trying to?

Everyone makes mistakes – even you – so get over it. You need to stop setting standards so high that you can never be happy with yourself. Tell big sis to lighten up as your regular standard is usually perfect for others.

❧ The 'I need to help everyone' sis ❧

This is where she encourages your need to help or fix the difficulties of others. Your big sis won't let you see or deal with your own needs – instead, she urges you to help others.

She won't let you say no – even when you need to look after yourself. Then, when it all gets too much, she tells you others are letting you down.

This big sis needs to be told to back off. You have needs and you are in danger of giving too much, almost giving foolishly. You can become proud of your giving disposition and get trapped there.

You need to know how and when to say no to others. There is nothing wrong in saying no to others when you feel that you are being taken advantage of in any way.

ஃ The 'over-competitive, obsessed ஃ by performance' sis

This big sis feeds your need to succeed and to be seen to succeed. She'll ask you if you think that was excellent enough. Did everyone notice how well you did? Are your accomplishments clear?

She pushes you on, making you do more – even when you are exhausted. She won't let you listen to your body and makes you keep going.

This big sis also needs to be told to back off. You need to begin to live in the present and to practice simply being. Your big sis is turning you into a 'human doing' as opposed to a human being and is looking at everything to see if it is an accomplishment. She will push you too deeply into wanting to be loved solely for what you do.

ஃ The 'I don't trust you' sis ஃ

This big sis feeds into your self doubt and makes you very suspicious of everyone and everything around you. She looks around and, in a flash, has imagined the worst possible scenario and seen every conceivable danger. She makes you wary of others and their motivations. She doesn't allow you to trust others too easily.

You need to give your big sis a very firm message that all will be well and that you need to trust yourself. You need to say that it is not necessary to anticipate every potential problem.

There is no need to scope out every person and place like Jack Bauer on the TV show called 24. Perhaps she can let you trust yourself and allow you to make your own judgments and mistakes.

The 'I am strong, powerful and in charge' sis

This big sis encourages your controlling, bossy tendencies. She asks you what you are doing about controlling your life and your environment. She sees people getting in the way and eggs you on to confront them. You can become very comfortable with anger and not see the discomfort of others.

This big sis is powerful and can stop you getting close to others. Therefore, she needs to be assured that people are not out to take advantage of you. It is not necessary to be on battle alert all the time. Maybe there is no need to wage battle every time.

Finding your own voice

The main point of looking at our big sis is to allow us to see through her and allow us to glimpse the observer in all of us. This is the inner, higher being. We are more than our worries, our doubts, our obsessions. Looking beyond the voice and having it recede allows you to escape from everyday thinking and acting, and is vital in achieving any real change in your life.

Make your body your temple

Give equal time to your mind and body. Look after yourself. Exercise and eat wisely. It's no good having a wonderful business idea if you are not healthy enough to carry it out.

Your health is your greatest asset. Once you are healthy, you can set any goals. So concentrate on preventative measures and stay healthy.

⤳ Look after yourself ⤶

What is it about us women that we have such a hard time looking after ourselves as well as looking after others? I wonder if you sometimes ask yourself "what about my needs?" or "what about my time?" Have you thought about how big a part guilt plays in this self forgetting?

I reckon women have an oversupply of guilt. Yes, I know we all try to equally apportion the tasks around the family but have you noticed how, when someone is sick, it is always mum who gets the call and has to change her schedule?

I think if you can crack this one, it will change your life. You need to look after yourself first, so that you can take care of others. You need to make a very positive contract with yourself and vow that you will always make your body your temple.

It all starts in the head with our thoughts, so the first adaptation is to lose the guilty thoughts now. It's not like you are on a vacation. When you have lessened the grip of the 'guilties,' then start a body temple plan to make sure you really do put yourself first.

❧ Temple builders ❧

The first practical place to start is with the people you live with. Here are some easy pointers to get you started:

Take time to get yourself excellent childcare

Worrying about your children while you are at work is one of the biggest energy drainers I know. I don't know how men do it, but they seem to be able to operate a series of separate boxes in their heads, home in one, work in another, friends in the third and sports in a special box. If you can't do this – and I know I can't – then you need to put your mind at rest.

Forget about being a domestic goddess

You must lower housework right down to the bottom of your priorities. Who cares if your house is less than perfect? In the grand scheme of things, your health is more important. I see so many women who look wretched, white in the face with exhaustion, but with sparkling windows!

Divide up the chores among the family

Make lists and dole out responsibility. Don't nag about different tasks. Instead, move to a different level and actually make people responsible for grocery shopping, cleaning, dog feeding, etc.

If the fridge is empty, the house dirty and the dog starving it's obvious to one and all who's responsible. At that stage, it is vital that you hold your nerve and not crack and go to the grocery store. Wait it out. Responsibility means responsibility.

Communicate your needs clearly

There is no reward for being a silent victim. Do you see silent women who suffer away minding everyone, right up until they either blow up or eventually succumb to illness?

I see no virtue in this and think it wiser to be honest and clear about your situation and to clearly ask for all the help you need. A lot of the time, we simply don't ask for help, so we can hardly complain when we are not offered any.

Live in the present

There is a great peace in living in the present. Sadly, I wear myself out making plans and anticipating the next problem and I envy women who float along trusting in the future. They live in the present moment and are usually calm and less stressed than me.

I have been practicing this notion of letting go and seeing what happens. Usually, I am delighted with the results and make a note of trying this approach more often. If like me you are an inveterate planner try giving your mind and body a rest and see what happens. It could be life changing.

Have time for yourself

If you don't slot in specific times for yourself in the week you can be certain that you will not have any 'me time.' Your own time is always the first to be dropped if you are busy.

When I say 'me time,' I mean time alone doing something you really like. I don't mean time with your partner or the gal pals. I mean all alone. If you choose a time in the week, the same time each week, and keep to it, then you will develop the habit.

You could say Saturday morning was your time and find that the family quickly gets used to the idea. Once you have allocated a given period, it is easy to spend the time enjoyably, e.g. having a massage, visiting shops, taking a long walk; maybe even just having a coffee and cake, sitting by the sea, or attending an art class. It's exciting thinking about it. Go on, have a go.

ᴥ Your health is your wealth ᴥ

There is no avoiding the really basic things that every woman needs to do to stay healthy. I keep reading about all kinds of elaborate plans, gadgets and diets that will change your life. They are all designed to fool you into thinking that if you buy them you will be in better shape. It's all nonsense. What you need is to pay attention to yourself, read the signs your body is giving you, and take the time to mind yourself. Our bodies talk to us all the time, telling us they are tired, hungry, stressed, and worn out: we just don't listen.

You probably know the basics already, but take time to check in with yourself and see if you are currently watching these basics.

Does your behavior enhance your health?

ᴥ Are you eating breakfast?	
ᴥ Do you eat little but often?	
ᴥ Do you know what constitutes a balanced diet?	
ᴥ Are you getting all five food groups?	
ᴥ Are you eating five portions of fruit and vegetables every day?	
ᴥ Are you on a diet or using common sense?	
ᴥ Are you actively watching your portion size at every meal?	
ᴥ Do you take exercise or a walk every day?	
ᴥ Are you getting enough sleep?	
ᴥ Do you take time out to relax?	

Don't waste your anger

Anger is the ruling passion in some people's
lives. Is it in yours? If so, use that anger wisely.

Anger, if used properly, can move mountains.
Don't squander it on winning petty points.
Always remember that although you are
comfortable with your anger, many other
people find it very distressing.

Anger is a powerful force and if used wisely can move mountains. If used
foolishly it leaves you exhausted, resentful and annoyed with yourself.

Is anger a key part of your life?

Ask yourself these questions to see if you are an angry person and if your
anger is a part of your being:

- Do I often feel a sense of personal injustice on behalf of others?
- Do I feel the need to do something to put it right?
- Am I able to leave a wrong 'unrighted'?
- Do I take action before I think?
- Do I feel the need to always say what I feel regardless of the situation?
- Do I take into account the reactions of others to my comments?
- Am I surprised by the strength of my feelings about things?
- Do I even notice others' reactions and, if so, do I think they are too soft-skinned?

These are questions to make you ponder. I find that people who are heavily
influenced by their gut as opposed to their head or their heart have strong
passion and anger flowing through their system.

✍ Triggers to anger ✍

Trigger: not coping

You can sometimes go around with a lot of small things bothering you. Each, in itself, is not the breaking point, but the sheer accumulation of them gets you down. You feel under pressure, you are worried and wondering how to cope, but still actually coping.

Then, along comes the proverbial last straw and the camel's back breaks. You cease to cope and you snap. Usually, it is because of something really insignificant like the lid off the toothpaste – again – or the dirty clothes strewn on the floor. Nothing serious, but as the last straw, it constitutes an inflammatory act. It is important to watch out for the signs of nearing the point of not coping and to ward off the meltdown.

Try stopping before you get exhausted, as coping ability diminishes dramatically with fatigue. Going to bed can be the perfect solution when you can no longer cope.

Trigger: response to someone else's anger

Have you ever felt yourself under attack from someone else's raw anger? Anyone working in a front line customer care position will tell you about it. Imagine being the person who announces another delay in a departing flight to an exhausted group of passengers at 11pm.

There is something visceral about another's anger pointed at you – you react before you even realise it. Even if you are caught off-guard, the ability to pull back from the reactive response is crucial. It is not good when we get upset and angry and it really has nothing to do with us.

It is a hazard in many jobs and you need to realise that it is the other person's issue – not yours – and that you do not need to respond.

It is amazing how many companies do not see how much of a drain these kinds of situations have on their staff and do not provide training on how to deal with them. If you regularly find yourself in this position, ask for help with it. You will be better at your job if you have this skill.

Trigger: lacking trust in those around you

Nothing builds up the stress levels more than working or living in a situation where you lack trust in those around you. Lack of trust wears you down eventually, corroding your ability to function well.

I have seen trust issues build up when people don't realise that trust has to be earned – not commanded – and that it is not easily earned. It comes over time and requires honest thought and action.

If you find yourself in a position where you don't trust those around you, especially their intent towards you, I suggest that you believe your instincts, as women's instincts on this are very accurate.

Be aware that this can set you up for anger. The underlying layers of mistrust weaken your defences and you can easily be triggered into an angry reaction. It's better to tackle the trust issues and clear them away – or simply leave. One way or the other, you are better off not being in a poisonous atmosphere.

Trigger: being ignored

There is nothing worse than being ignored and being made to feel that you are not contributing. Over time, being ignored can affect your self-confidence and wear it down. It is often a tactic used in bad management when the manager does not know what to do, so they take the easiest (for them) approach and act as if you were not there.

Have you seen this in action? Do you know the signs? Someone is targeted and they find they don't get memos or emails. Meetings take place and they are not invited, outings take place without them and are discussed the next day. It is like being invisible.

If this is not tackled in a forthright and professional way, it can result in a blow up, which usually ends up badly for the victim who has been manoeuvred into angry and unprofessional behavior. Watch for the signs and be clear and coolheaded – thoughtful and detached behavior is crucial in eliminating this kind of intimidating conduct.

Beware the triggers

If you fall victim to these triggers and react angrily, you are wasting your passion. You are allowing others to control you. The power of your anger is not being used for good – or for your reasons; you are being a puppet and reacting to outside stimuli.

Remember that people are very good at manipulation and they can quickly figure out your triggers and use them for their own purposes.

Anger can do surprising good, especially if it is yours and not just a reaction to a trigger, and comes from a good source. It can give you energy and drive and bring you to levels of excellence.

It sets you apart as someone with a mission who has the passion and energy to accomplish something. It is a completely different force to negative reactive anger. It is vital to know your anger and use it wisely. Don't give control of it to someone else.

Don't harbor resentments

Holding onto resentments is like carrying around a jar of corrosive acid inside you. If you are knocked off balance it spills over and hurts you.

Give away the resentments. Move on. Don't give your precious energy and vitality to bad feelings located in the past. Feelings and happenings over which you no longer have control. They are over so let them go.

What is resentment?

Have you ever felt angry about something and then felt that you have suffered an injustice? I'm sure you have, as it happens all the time. The key point is that when you continue to hold onto that anger, it develops into the far more poisonous feeling of resentment.

Anger is a frequent event, as when someone provokes you or you are upset by someone's actions. Understanding the causes of anger and your way of dealing with it are an important part of coping with life. Anger is justified, but you need to become aware of your anger. You must accept it, deal with it, learn how to quickly dispel it and not allow it to control you.

Resentment comes from unresolved anger

It builds up in this way:

- Feeling attacked
- Visceral reaction in our body
- Rush to self-protection
- Thoughts go to planning defensive actions
- Attack strategies are planned
- Thinking about it

- Sublimating desire to attack
- Turning anger inside and harboring it
- Unresolved anger festers
- The hurt remains
- You get used to the feeling of unresolved anger and you nourish the hurt

You have now developed a full-blown resentment.

Distinguish between new and old anger

If you have been carrying around your anger for days or weeks – in some cases years – you have a bad case of old anger causing resentment. It can get a grip on your whole life and color all your interactions with others. It is a truly corrosive force.

 # Conquering resentment

Understanding your anger

A real breakthrough comes if you can realise what has really made you angry. Being truthful with yourself is hard, but in the quiet of your own mind think carefully about what is really going on. Detach yourself from what others think and be brutally frank with yourself.

Identify the underlying emotion

Anger is usually masking hurt or fear – or both. You are deeply hurt by what the other person has said or done, you may feel they have attacked you and harmed you. Hurt is causing the lingering feeling – not anger.

Sometimes, we are really fearful of the consequences of the anger. Fear is blinding us. Someone might leave us or expose us. If you really think it through, you may come to see the underlying cause and then you can really tackle it.

Gain perspective

When you are trapped in your own view of things, it can become a real prison and you lose perspective. You need detachment to put things into a proper perspective. If you are inclined to take things personally, it is vital to regularly perform a sanity check with another person whose detachment you trust.

I have a number of friends who I know will give me honest feedback when I ask them for it. We often say to each other "let's reframe the situation." We look at what happened from a number of perspectives, always giving the other side the benefit of the doubt. I encourage you to develop that kind of support group around you, to allow you to get precious outside assessment.

This is really vital today when so many businesses are in trouble. You may be under severe stress at work and need the input of people outside your immediate workplace to do a good sanity check.

Cultivate detachment

You must never take yourself too seriously or take anything personally. We are all inclined to think we occupy the center of the universe, but really we are only the center of our own tiny universe. I have found it to be a good rule to keep asking myself if this is really as serious as it seems. Bad things happen, but we can really take many minor incidents way too seriously, blowing them out of all proportion. So what if someone is late or misses a deadline? There is always time – it is not the end of the world.

I remember early in my career working for a man who taught me great detachment, although teaching me that lesson was far from his mind. He used to appear beside my desk in an incandescent rage, no matter what the issue. His favorite phrase was "this is white hot urgent," no matter what the task.

All of our team quickly learnt the art of detachment in order to survive his misplaced urgency and his mania. We simply discounted down his urgency to a more normal level. He lost all our respect and it was impossible to really have an emergency, as we were worn out with the fake ones.

Detaching yourself and not getting caught up in the wake of crazy-making people is vital. If you feed off others' craziness, it can prolong your feelings of hurt and fear.

Don't take too many things personally. I find people rarely get out of bed with the aim of hurting me. I am often caught in the collateral of other people's actions, but it is not meant for me personally. I may just be in the wrong place at the wrong time. If you are nursing resentment towards someone, you can get caught and take something personally, even if it has nothing to do with you. You take it to fertilise your festering resentment.

Forgive and move on

The biggest cure for resentment is to take out the cause of your fear or hurt and give it some air. Really examine it and be honest with yourself. Ask yourself what it would mean to you to let it go. Also ask yourself the opposite question – what is it giving me if I continue to hold on to it?

Pen and paper are your best tools. Write out all the angles.

- Why are you angry?
- With whom are you angry?
- Is it a justified anger?
- Is it really anger or fear and hurt?
- List your fears and hurts
- Examine them in a detached manner
- Can you let them go?
- How would you feel if you did let them go?
- How is holding on to them making you feel?
- Distinguish between the two feelings

You will come to an answer. Remember that the destination is forgiveness. You can only really escape resentment when you let go and forgive the other person.

Take the power back to you as resentment only really weakens you and gives control of your life to someone else. What a waste!

Withdraw from negativity

If you find your energy being drained by negative people, even those close to you, it's vital to temporarily withdraw and recharge your batteries. You cannot thrive in an environment where you are being leeched of energy.

First remove the energy drainers and then consciously begin to refill your energy.

You become what you think, so be careful what thoughts you cultivate. Quite simply, your thoughts can rule your life; they can make it or break it. It is no accident that all the self-development books on the market today consciously and repeatedly emphasise the power of positive thinking.

They know that this is the way for you to take control of your life's outcomes. That is a simple enough concept, but I think that the first step of getting away from negativity can be overlooked. I want you to have a conscious strategy in place for dealing with the negativity in your life.

It would be foolish to think that we can just ward off negativity with a wave of our hand. It is an ever-present and self-replicating force in our lives today. Some people delightedly feed off the decline in our economies. I know certain media commentators have made negativity and 'I told you so' their hallmark.

So if we accept that it is always going to be there and that the present circumstances are feeding it, then it is prudent to have thought out a personal strategy for withdrawing from it.

Your personal strategy for withdrawing from negativity

Action: realise the adverse power of negative thinking

First, realise the power of continuous negative thinking. Always thinking the worst can totally influence the way you feel and act. It can become a self-fulfilling prophecy. The more you think you are not good enough, the less good you feel and act.

The more you think your business is in trouble, the more difficult it becomes to do business. The less you think of yourself, the more you will inevitably find fault with yourself.

Action: make a conscious effort to break your negative thinking habits

Realise if you are in a one-thought pattern and break it. Our thoughts go around in cycles and if constantly negative can drive us down into a form of depression. Take a reality check on your thoughts; discuss them with someone to get an outside perspective. It may not be as bad as you think.

A good way to rebalance is to start and end each day with a blindingly positive thought. How about waking up and telling yourself you are fabulous? Try it and see if you can get that wonderful thought in first, then compare it to the negative ones.

Every night as you go to sleep, review your day and try to turn all the negatives into positives. I do this a lot now to counteract the depressing news all around me.

Action: first recognize negativity at source

Negativity comes in the guise of pragmatism. People say that they are merely being practical or pragmatic when they tell you your job prospects are slim, your business will struggle, and your stress levels will rise.

They are not being sensible as they completely discount any power that you have and make you a victim of outside forces. You must separate opinion from fact. Never take on board mere opinions as you do not know what prejudices or personal baggage are fuelling these opinions.

Action: cut off the inflow of negativity

The main source of negativity can be the people you are surrounded by each day. It only takes one 'negatroid' droning in your ear to bring you down. I call them psychic vampires and the only answer is to get away from them as fast as possible.

Don't believe everything the media tells you and don't rely on any one source for your news. They are all coming from a certain subjective perspective. So pick and choose and make up your own mind. If it is all too much and the constant negativity is getting you down, turn it off.

Action: don't concentrate on negativity

Don't get stuck in a rut when something bad happens. You must not give your full attention to rehashing the negative, as all your power and will to change can be drained away. It is amazing how powerful a drainer of energy negative thought can be.

Make it a rule to always look for the opposite viewpoint. If you say to yourself "I will never get another job," try reframing it and saying "This could be an opportunity to change careers, to try something new."

Action: make negativity visible

Negativity can be a pernicious, invisible force. It can hang around people, organizations, families, groups, and permeate their every fibre, yet be totally invisible to them. Have you ever felt a really negative vibration when you meet some people or go into a certain room?

I often find I can pick up the negative energy when I go into an office with a lot of industrial relations problems. It permeates the atmosphere.

It is vital to make this negativity visible to all involved so that it can be solved. Look out for your wellbeing. Check and see if you are part of an invisible negativity. Even one person recognizing it and breaking through the pattern can have a big effect.

You read a lot about corporate values today and how the lack of them has gotten us into the mess we are in. I think that people found themselves prisoners of negative forces and were unable to stand up and stop the force. The position of whistleblower can be a lonely one.

✎ Beware our bias to remembering ✎ the negative

Oddly, our minds focus on and remember the negatives more than the positives in our lives. Have you ever noticed how people remember insults and put-down comments, often retelling the story in intimate detail many years later?

One of my sisters used to tell a story of how our other sister borrowed some very special clothes from her 'bottom drawer' then wore them and hid them to avoid being found out. Unfortunately, the hidden stash was found and all hell broke lose. She could tell that story to her grandchildren with the fresh hurt as if it had happened that very day.

In my native Ireland, girls used to prepare for marriage by filling the bottom drawer of their dresser with special clothes for their wedding day and for the honeymoon. It was a very special undertaking and cost precious money to fill it up at a time when money was scarce. It is easy to see that taking from that collection was, indeed, a huge crime. The many positive experiences did not get remembered as well or retold as often in our house.

Being aware of this bias can help us maintain objectivity and should encourage us not to mentally give priority to the negative things that happen in our lives.

✎ Lifesavers in combating negativity ✎

- ✎ Turn off the drip feed of negativity in your life
- ✎ Immerse yourself in positive people and positive reading
- ✎ Break the cycle of thinking
- ✎ Reframe all negative thoughts
- ✎ Meditate

- ✎ Stop being hard on yourself
- ✎ Stop thinking in absolutes
- ✎ Constantly pay attention to your filters, don't let one bad incident ruin the rest of your day

Surround yourself with enriching people

When you are positive, you attract positive people to you. To thrive, you must build a circle of positive, caring, enrichers around you. Write down their names now. Spend more time with them.

You can't have negative people around you

You need to do something to counteract the current unrelenting media barrage of negativity coming at you. If you were to listen to the media and not take counter actions, you would sink without trace in a sea of pundits and commentators.

The very best action you can take is to get rid of all the negative people in your life and surround yourself with enriching people. Enrichers are the people who, although they understand the realities of economic life, nevertheless remain positive and upbeat in their outlook. They are not Pollyanna people, who are unreasonably positive – they are people who choose to retain a 'can do' attitude even when things are difficult.

Now more than ever before, we need to gather all our resources to stay on top. I am sure you feel like getting under your bed covers and staying there some days, but the problem is that you have to come out eventually and the longer you stay under, the longer and harder the journey back to normality.

Take a look around at the people you spend your days with. Ask yourself these questions:

- Do they have no effect on my mood?
- Do they lift my mood or drop it further?
- When I leave them, do I feel better or worse?

If you feel they are not lifting you or are draining your energy, you need to limit your exposure to them and protect yourself when you are with them.

Find the enrichers in your life

When you limit the negative people, you open up a whole new space for enrichers to come into your life. These are people who have a positive approach to life, who radiate powerful energy and who leave you feeling better about yourself and your life.

They do not drain you – they have no need to. They are so self-sufficient they are able to reach out and energise you. They are a rare breed – but they do exist.

One of life's great mysteries is that when you switch off negativity and go positive, the enrichers appear. They hate negativity and are wise enough to stay away from it. If you are negative, you attract more negativity, but if you are positive, you attract more positivity.

You are who you mix with, you take on board the attitudes of the people you spend your time with, so be careful. You need to know how to recognize enrichers so that you can include more of them in your sphere.

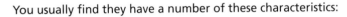 How do you recognize an enricher?

You usually find they have a number of these characteristics:

They use action words

Listen to their vocabulary. Take President Obama: Yes, we can. That gives you a clue. Do you hear lots of verbs? If you do, you are in the presence of a 'doer' as verbs denote action.

Listen out for the following words: *can, do, move, increase, tackle, strive, achieve, plan, work, grow* and *overcome.*

They have high energy levels

Is the person full of energy and vitality? Do they move the molecules in a room when they enter? Do their eyes sparkle? Do people perk up when they are around? Do people look forward to their visit? How do children react to them?

They have high happiness levels

Are they happy people? I find unhappy people are rarely able to escape their own problems long enough to enrich you. They need you to be their enrichers. That's okay, but this is a hunt for your enrichers.

They have a low moan index

It is useful to gauge how much moaning someone does before they take action about the problem. We are all entitled to a good moan every now and again – it's a sanity device.

However, for me the key point is how long and how often people moan about the same thing and yet take no action. If the person loves the sound of their own exquisite moaning voice, you are lost. There will be no enriching coming from them.

They are good listeners

Enrichers listen attentively so they can understand the issue you are facing. They wait patiently until you are finished and don't rush to unburden a bigger problem onto you. They don't play that game of telling you a bigger problem to diminish yours. They don't say "don't worry about losing your job, I am worse off, I lost my job and my house and my dog and cat." They don't talk your problem away.

They have good questioning skills

Enrichers ask good questions because they want to understand the real issues so they can help you in a practical and useful way. Watch the questions people ask. See if they use who, what, why, where and when. If they use these open questions, they are really trying to help you.

They have a grown up approach to life

Enrichers are grown-up people who have developed away from the selfishness and petulance of teenage years. There are a lot of fully-grown adults whose development has arrested at 16.5 years. To be an enricher, you need to be able to see beyond your own needs and moods.

✺ Give more than you take ✺

Sadly, I find the world can be divided into the two camps; enrichers or takers. People in a rush and on the way up the ladder of success are rarely enrichers. They are too focussed on their future and what you can do for them. The difficult times we find ourselves in are causing an epidemic of these takers. When people start to panic, they only see their own survival and not yours.

Don't answer questions, respond to them

Don't ever feel you have to quickly answer questions, especially ones about your private life or your dreams.

Look behind the question and see what the other person really wants to know or do. You may misunderstand the question. Focus on the intent behind the question. It's more revealing.

People ask too many questions

'Curiosity killed the cat.' The well-known proverb serves as a warning that sometimes people can be too questioning for their own good.

I am amazed at how openly curious people can be and how they can probe and pry into other's lives. Sometimes I think it is just idle curiosity and there is no harm in it, yet I don't feel you should be put under pressure to answer every question you are asked.

Look behind questions to their real purpose and then decide how much you are prepared to say. I am amused by some people who seem to carry around a veritable questionnaire in their head, always ready to be pulled out. Don't feel under pressure to fill in other people's questionnaires.

✐ Probe before you answer ✐

Here are my favorite probing questions to ask to allow you to respond rather than reactively answer.

- ✐ Can you tell me more?
- ✐ Can you explain?
- ✐ What exactly do you mean by…?
- ✐ What is the essence of that …?
- ✐ Before I answer, can you clarify…?
- ✐ So what I hear you saying is….
- ✐ This is what I heard you saying, did I understand correctly?

✐ When visioning, don't answer ✐ questions – respond to them

When I am working with women and they are going through the delicate phase of visioning their future, they can be very unsure of themselves, as they are projecting forward to envisage the life and career they would like to build for themselves. This is a time for introspection and takes courage and a very positive attitude.

This expansive and positive mindset is a precious state and can be completely destroyed by the wrong conversation. Early on in my work on the SHOES program, I watched women leave a SHOES session completely fired up and ready to push their boundaries then come back the next week completely deflated with a list a mile long of all the negatives.

They had shared their dream with someone who asked too many negative questions – and they had answered them all. They had not kept their counsel. I always tell the people who do my SHOES program to deflect questions about their thinking until they are really ready.

I suggest that they go behind the questions and see if the person is really interested in helping them and to probe for information without revealing their innermost fledgling ideas. Sometimes, the person can be an enricher and a source of inspiration, but sometimes they can be a psychic vampire waiting to pounce. So be careful and don't feel the need to satisfy idle curiosity.

❧ In interviews, don't answer ❧ questions – respond to them

Often in interviews you can be asked a question and you naturally feel you are expected to answer it exactly as it was asked. Don't. You will fail to do yourself justice. A lot of people who end up in interview positions have no training for the task and ask very imprecise questions.

If you spend time answering them, as asked, you can get lost and fail to make the best impression through no fault of your own. I suggest that a far better strategy is to take time out to think, look behind the question and try to figure out exactly what the person wants to know.

A very good example was when a client I was mentoring went for an interview for a CEO position in a national charity. The foundation was funded by private donations, so understanding the whole area of philanthropy and the best fundraising strategies was a key requirement for the candidate.

One of the people on the interview panel was a dedicated member of the Board and clearly his brief on the interview was to probe the candidate's expertise in fundraising. My client was indeed quite skilled in this area but the questions asked did not initially allow her to prove her worth.

The questions were about who she knew and who her contacts were. All questions which showed that the Board member felt that who you knew was a crucial factor in fundraising.

My client remembered the phrase 'Don't answer questions, respond to them' and before answering, took her time to go behind and probe what precisely the interviewer wanted to know.

She was able to reframe the question into "Do you want to know if I have a strategy for fundraising your target" and to prove from her career examples that she did have excellent strategies. The interviewer was delighted with the clarification of his question and the positive answers. Yes, you will be pleased to hear that she got the job.

Don't answer questions – respond to them. The rules:

- Pause before answering
- Spend longer thinking than talking
- Clarify before answering
- Reframe the question so you really understand
- Answer a question with a question
- Challenge the question
- Challenge the right to ask the question
- If all else fails, be vague
- Don't feed the idle curiosity of others

I love to recall the words on curiosity as written by Oscar Wilde, the Irish poet.

"The public have an insatiable curiosity to know everything, except what is worth knowing."

Beware resistance

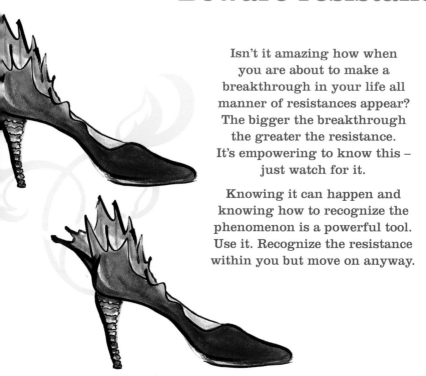

Isn't it amazing how when you are about to make a breakthrough in your life all manner of resistances appear? The bigger the breakthrough the greater the resistance. It's empowering to know this – just watch for it.

Knowing it can happen and knowing how to recognize the phenomenon is a powerful tool. Use it. Recognize the resistance within you but move on anyway.

I wonder if you are like me and spend ages examining all the angles before you decide to change, but then when you have made the decision, you want the change to occur as fast as possible. You completely forget how long the pros and cons phase actually took.

Recently, I have begun to notice a phenomenon that takes place in the 'I want the change now' phase. Have you ever noticed it too? It's as if once the decision is made to change something in your life, a strange form of resistance appears. I have watched this resistance occur to me and to many of the women I work with.

⤷ Change invites resistance ⤶

Have a look at the following and see if any of them apply to you or remind you of recent changes in your life.

Have you

- ⤷ Decided to start a new business and found that your old one starts to get busier?
- ⤷ Finally decided to leave the boring job and then your employer offers you something more interesting?
- ⤷ Eventually worked up the courage to leave a relationship and the person seems to have a personality change for the better?
- ⤷ Bravely handed in your notice at work and they suddenly appreciate you and offer you a raise?

⤷ The level of resistance matches ⤶ the change

My experience tells me that the bigger the change, the bigger the resistance will be. Weird, but I take this to be a strange way of testing your determination. I ask lots of people about this and I find there is a trend which suggests that really big changes can precipitate a matching level of angst and drag.

I suggest to people that they take heart, as the huge resistance may perversely be indicating that it is the very thing they need to do at this moment in time. It could represent a wonderful turning point for them.

This very thing happened to me. When I decided to refocus my business a number of years ago to build the SHOES concept by working primarily with women, this resistance showed up big-time. With no prompting on my part, I began to receive tenders for work from a lot of organizations – they wanted me to do the kind of consultancy I had done in previous years. Two things struck me. The first was the big number of offers of work for what I wanted to leave behind and secondly the fact that they were from the type of clients I had been angling to land for some time.

ᴖ My experience of resistance ᴖ

During the previous year I would have walked over broken glass to land a number of these clients. But I had moved on and made my decision to start something new and exciting. I wanted to leave the safe behind and the safe was pursuing me.

I thought about this a lot and finally saw it as a test of my determination to move in the new, more challenging direction. The test was this: if I was still not sure about my new direction, I could take all this work and postpone the new focus. It would be a huge, cuddly comfort blanket that I could snuggle into and not have to take the risk associated with the new initiative. Boy, was that resistance tough to overcome!

Think of your own recent change and see if you can identify the signs of the accompanying resistance. What is the change and what is the resistance?

ᴖ Watch how you behave ᴖ

You can generate a lot of the resistance by the way you behave and the signals you send out. If you go around openly discussing your new big step with everyone, then you should not be surprised if you get mixed reactions to your plans. People usually react based on their own fears, not yours.

You can collect a lot of unnecessary collateral and confound yourself with differing and opposing opinions which you have to work your way through. You bring grief upon yourself as you talk to the negative ones to see why they are negative. You then need to talk to the positive ones to recover from the negative ones, and on and on it goes: a lovely big resistance-generating machine.

See how you can self-generate a big amount of resistance just by canvassing a lot of extraneous opinion. Imagine where you would be if you had just gone and started the project and applied all that energy to it. So how do you deal with this resistance? Sometimes you have to say to yourself that this may be the time to leap and go with the new and exciting idea.

❧ Leap anyway, with due preparation ❧

Change can look as if you are leaping into something and your courage may depend on how well you examined all the options beforehand. I believe we should not jump blindly into things but should examine all the angles first. I have seen people set up businesses on blind faith and go bust.

During my twenty years spent in the not-for-profit sector I have seen many people in voluntary agencies launch campaigns to help vulnerable people – with tragic consequences. They leapt and others suffered. Individuals can set up charities very easily and leap into fundraising, all because they want to help. They need to do something. They don't think about realities like logistics, personnel or appropriateness of the aid.

If the resistance is merely second thoughts about the wisdom of your decision, then deal with the second thoughts but don't let them bring about a state of paralysis.

This was aptly illustrated by the poet W.H. Auden in his poem Leap Before You Look:

The sense of danger must not disappear
The way is certainly both short and steep
However gradual it looks from here
Look if you like, but you will have to leap

Don't get stuck by resistance but leap with your eyes open.

Be realistic with yourself

Set yourself up for success by making realistic goals. Take into account the amount of time, energy and finances you have when setting the goals. Be realistic. Imagine the feeling of success when you check them off your list.

However, don't set yourself up for failure by expecting too much of yourself. We are often our own hardest critic.

❧ Be informed before you set goals ❧

If you go off doing something with inadequate research, acting on a whim you are definitely setting yourself up for failure. It is a mistake to confuse optimistic drive with headstrong folly. Do your homework........so easy today on the internet.

Sometimes a quick conversation with someone who has been down the path before you will be invaluable. If possible find an expert and ask for advice.

❧ Don't set unrealistic ❧ short term goals

The basic principles of goal setting are simple to understand but what eludes a lot of people is keeping them realistic so that you have every chance of success.

I find many people are overly ambitious in the short term and not ambitious in the long term. Entrepreneurs at the early stages of the business set up are impatient to be trading and have the product out in the market place. They have huge expectations of themselves for the first few weeks and months. They rush to sell, setting unrealistic sales targets.

They over-estimate the immediate future. In contrast their middle to long range growth figures are vague. Failure comes as a huge shock, but sadly the initial rush to succeed caused the failure.

Setting a goal that is obviously impossible to achieve is not only foolish, but will end up frustrating you to the point where you may give up on your goals.

❧ Set your own goals ❧

I suggest that you look at your present goals and double check that they are your goals.

Too often we allow others to have undue influence and to set our goals. I can't tell you how many women tell me thay are losing weight because their husband said they were too fat. They were on a long long diet as they were always failing. They had no intrinsic, internal motivation. They were living someone elses goal. If you find yourself in that position, reassess.

❧ Realistically appraise your fears ❧

Don't set a goal so large and awesome that you frighten yourself into stunned inactivity. By all means have a big audacious aim in your life and reach for the sky but be sure to set reasonable achievable goals to get you there. Then focus on one goal at a time, remember every step is a step forward.

❧ Be aware of three driving forces ❧ in your behavior

It is useful to be aware of these three driving forces as this will help you gain another level of self knowledge and help you set realistic expectations for your behavior. It is sensible to be realistic in what you expect of yourself.

A useful insight comes from the enneagram (called enneagram of personality) studies which note that each of us has an element of the following three types of behavior; self preservation, social and one-to-one behaviors. It notes that we all have an element of each but most people's behavior is predominantly led by one type.

Have a look at the three types and decide which is your dominant type.

Self-preservation behavior

Our self preservation behavior comes into play to ensure our personal survival and addresses issues like protection, safety, security, our comfort, and sufficient amounts of food, shelter and warmth.

A person who is heavily in self preserve behavior will look for food at regular times, need enough sleep, generally not tolerate discomfort and will look after their own needs first.

If you recognise yourself in this then you need to be realistic about setting yourself up for long hours of work or long travel schedules. Be aware of your own needs in this regard as overlooking them is unrealistic.

Social behavior

Our social behavior comes into play when we find ourselves in groups .

We have an urge to live in groups and be sociable, but clearly we differ in how comfortable we are in groups. A social person's energy goes to issues related to membership or participation in groups or communities. People who are social are very comfortable in groups of people and have a remarkable ability to work a crowd.

They read groups and have no difficulty moving between people. They dread getting caught with one person and are the type who is looking, over your shoulder while talking to you, seeing who else they might meet.

One-to-one behavior

One-to-one behavior is when we find ourselves in a one-to-one situation. Some people are most comfortable when in a one to one conversation and consider an evening a success if they meet one interesting person. In contrast a social person would consider that hell.

The real benefit of being a one-to-one is that you are very engaging on an individual level and other one-to-ones love you. However, you can be too intense for a social or self preserve person.

It is a useful insight to know that you may not be good in groups and that there is nothing wrong in that. You need to be aware of that and not overly force yourself into that situation.

Similiarly, knowing you're 'self-preservation' is important to you as it allows you to preplan when you will eat and drink on long journeys. Knowing you have a tendency to like one-on-one interactions allows you to monitor yourself and make a special effort to not get stuck with one person.

You need to take that into account when you are planning your social and work schedules.

Life is too short for regrets

What is the point of regretting
things? It is a huge waste of your
valuable energy. You can spend a lot
of your valuable energy regretting
past actions, rerunning things
through your mind again and again.

You look backwards and try to change
things. How futile is that?
You can't change the past.
Get over it. Move on.

Do you ever have regrets? What are they and what brought them about?
If you are having regrets at the moment, I would like you to reconsider
this. I would like you to adopt a new mantra: life is much too short for
regretting things.

I would like to suggest to you that regretting things is a huge waste of
your valuable energy.

～ Things undone ～

Like you, I see people who spend a lot of their life carrying around a set of regrets about things they have not done in their life. They fail to see that life always has possibilities. The only problems are in their own minds.

I was shocked recently when a friend who is in her fifties told me that she regretted not going to college and studying more. I asked her if she had considered doing some evening courses to see how she felt about returning to education.

She told me that it would be impossible as she was too old for that, the time had passed. She sounded as if she believed her days were numbered. She was more comfortable living with her regret than doing something about it.

I found it profoundly saddening as we had gone to school together and I certainly didn't feel like I was ready for the scrapheap and, although she didn't realise it, nor was she.

～ Missed opportunities ～

How many people get on in years, look back and say "is that all there is?" or "is that it?" They feel that somehow they have missed out on life. They regret all the places they did not visit.

They regret not learning to ski or windsurf while they had the energy and did not feel too old and creaky. Are these regrets good? I wonder what use they serve.

There is always time to reboot your life, time to learn a sport, even if it's a gentler one. I am full of admiration for retiring couples who sell off all their possessions, say goodbye to the cold north and head for sunny, light and warm places. They cheerfully start all over again, no regrets or looking back.

☙ Missed relationships ❧

I think the saddest regrets are when people regret their failure to develop and protect their most valuable relationships. They regret all the time they spent working to build a career or a business – and not with their family.

They turn around one day and their family is grown up. High achieving alpha men and women see their work and affluence as their driving forces when they are young.

They will often tell you they are doing it for their family. They work 18-hour days, 7 days a week for their family. Sure they do! I just don't believe it. They do it for themselves. Their regrets are sad to see.

Their families have become so used to fending for themselves that they go on without them. Quite often, when the workaholic retires and looks for time with their family, they are no longer there.

This is a developing problem now for corporate workers as the old rules no longer apply. Giving your soul to the company no longer means anything; the rules of loyalty have changed irreversibly.

Huge companies are closing overnight and people are asking themselves why they sacrificed so much of their own private life to a company which does not value it. This is a lesson of our times and one which we should take to heart. Your life is indeed too short and too important to give to any employer.

☙ Horrible wake-up calls ❧

Great regrets can come around when you receive one of those horrible wake-up calls like the death of a loved one or a serious illness. People become introspective and start examining everything. They wonder "what if?" They start regretting all the missed opportunities to be with people, to experience friendship and love.

They see all the places they will not visit, the anniversaries that will not be celebrated. You wonder why we don't think about these issues before we get the horrible news. Life really is too short to miss out on love and friendship.

✎ Lives lived and unlived ✎

I attended two very sad funerals of friends who had died prematurely in their fifties in the recent past. I was struck by the difference in the remembrances people had of their interactions with the two men. For one, everyone spoke of their strong connection to this person. They spoke of his energy, his vitality, and his infectious love of life.

His purpose seemed to be tied to his ability to reach out, to connect and to bring joy. He was much loved and sadly missed by a large number of people. I never saw so many adults crying openly as I did at his funeral.

In contrast, the other funeral remembered a quiet, withdrawn, silent person. He was someone who lived in a quiet, reserved, tight group. He was not one to reach out freely to people beyond his inner circle.

He passed on quietly with few ripples on the pond. I found it hard to define his life's purpose or if he had achieved it. Oddly, I felt sadder at his passing as I felt he had not known his life's purpose and had passed through with little impact.

Find your life's purpose and aim to have no regrets.

Have clear boundaries

Women can have great crossover between different aspects of their lives. They are so good at multi-tasking that they blur the boundaries between personal and professional issues.

You leave yourself open to negative influences when your personal space is wide open. Keep your personal and professional spaces separate.

✎ We all have a personal boundary ✎

Your personal boundary is the space around you which is yours alone. It allows you to have a crystal clear idea of who you are and what you are doing. When you decide to allow someone inside your boundary, into your mental, physical and emotional space, you are opening your boundary.

✍ Maintaining a boundary ✍

The purpose of having clear boundaries is that you can take really good care of yourself. It is essential in today's world when we are under so much pressure that we set up an inner place where we can be safe. A crucial component of a healthy relationship is a strong personal boundary.

Ask yourself whether or not you are good at maintaining your personal space. How permeable is your boundary? For example, if your children ask you to take them out somewhere and you are exhausted and need to stop, what do you do?

If you are full of guilt about saying no then you may have personal boundary concerns. If you feel that your work colleagues are not pulling their weight and dumping on you, but you are suffering in silence then again you have a personal boundary concern.

✍ The internal boundary ✍

Recently, I have begun to question the delight we women take in being brilliant multi-taskers, mainly because of the very real cost to our personal space. I feel we have been eroding our own personal boundaries.

Have you ever found yourself having a number of conversations at once, doing three separate things at the same time and generally operating at many levels simultaneously? Do you find yourself forgetting your own needs and ending up exhausted at the end of the day?

While the benefits of multi-tasking are huge – as you get a lot done and come across as very effective – the downside is a personal one: often a hidden personal one. You often lose a clear sense of where your boundaries are as, in the effort to achieve so much, you allow your inner boundaries to be breached.

You can forget to maintain your inner personal boundary and allow work worries into your inner sanctum. You take work home, you never stop thinking about other issues and you simply make yourself sick.

Have a look at the boundary between you as a person and the things that you do. Is it clear enough? If you can't see a difference between you and your accomplishments, you need to address this.

✒ The external boundary ✒

Have you ever found yourself in a situation where you felt you were being told too much information about a person's life? They were sharing too much detail about their relationships, the inner details about who did and said what. If so, you are with someone who has boundary issues.

Do you think you might be doing this yourself? If you think that you are having problems keeping people at the right boundary level or you are not sure what the boundary is, you can try this wonderfully simple mechanism. In today's stressed world, it is useful to imagine that all the people who are making demands on you are stars rotating around your central axis. They are in your orbit: family, friends, co-workers, neighbours, random strangers, the delivery man, whoever.

You can't possibly deal with them all with the same intensity and pay equal attention to their demands. You would be exhausted if you tried, yet I see many women trying to achieve this level of equal interaction.

Instead, try adopting the inner and outer circle approach. It is very simple and works like this. You get pen and paper, draw a circle and put your name in it. Then draw a series of ever bigger circles out from the center, each one encapsulating the last. You are now looking at a set of ever increasing circles.

You need an inner one for the innermost circle of those most intimate to you and you work out through the circles.

- ✒ Partner, spouse, children, or parents
- ✒ A circle for trusted confidantes
- ✒ Close friends
- ✒ Friends
- ✒ Acquaintances
- ✒ Random people

You now write in one circle the names of everyone that you come into contact with and have a look at where people land. Clearly, you will have the least problem deciding where your closest people go but it can be very revealing to see where other people end up.

∽ Confused boundaries ∾

For example, when I have people do this exercise in family businesses, it works a treat. I did this recently with a family where the mother and father had run the business for years and the two sons and one daughter had worked in the business. Over the years, a number of trusted employees had become senior managers.

The boundary lines were very confused as the family discussed the business at home, leaving the senior managers out of the loop. The father discussed the children with the managers, often referring to inappropriate personal issues. The mother discussed her marriage problems with anyone who would listen to her, from delivery man to customer.

I was working with the mother and father who were at the top and were setting the whole tone for the company. Everyone was looking to them for direction and for the standards of behavior. We did the circle exercise and it was an eye opener for them as they had absolutely no idea that they had no boundaries and that certain conversations needed to remain within the innermost circle. They treated everyone as if they were all intimate members of one big family. They represent the different boundaries you are going to maintain around your personal space. You must make clear distinctions around each.

Find your inner space, define the boundary wall and be brave and assertive enough to maintain it.

Winter

I really feel that it is vital to practice the art of being; it is a huge part of my Celtic viewpoint to have time to simply be. When I was growing up, there was always an open fire in our living room and it was kept lit all winter long and was the focal point of our home.

Many homes in rural Ireland still have this, but alas it is falling victim to our busy life style. It was our center point and it encouraged the practice of staring into the fire and thinking. It encouraged us to sit and think and not to feel guilty about being quiet.

I feel that, in our lives today, we are becoming more and more action orientated and we are failing to pay attention to our need for regeneration. We simply do not make time to stop and rest. We undervalue the regenerative power of silence and time out alone. We fail to protect our inner essence and our positive energy.

Even nature takes a break

Winter is the time when nature takes a break and slows down. Growth stops and animals hibernate and wait for spring. It is an indoors time with lengthening nights and shortening days, and in many cultures, it ends with ceremonies recognizing rebirth.

One of my favorite leadership gurus is Peter Drucker and he is a fountain of common sense. I like his thoughts on reflection quoted here.

"Follow effective action with quiet reflection. From the quiet reflection will come even more effective action"

I find that we can become so focused on actions that we forget we need more than endless action – we need thoughtful considered action. To get this, we need to take time out to reflect on our past actions in order to get a positive outlook, to see where we really get our energy, to realize the preciousness of every single day and to plan how to avoid negativity.

The inhospitable weather of winter can keep you indoors and so give you the gift of perhaps one of the most precious commodities of this frantic age. Please take the winter Shoeisms as your chance to carve out this time and allow you see the true value of finding your time and place of tranquility.

You deserve peace and quiet. Please use the winter Shoeisms to take stock and to refocus on the positives in your life while making a plan to remove the negatives, so that you concentrate on your innermost priorities.

Never live from a scarcity perspective

Work up your very own abundance catcher and walk away from the scarcity 'glass half empty' people.

Conserve your inner essence

You only have so much energy – so you need to conserve it. This Shoeism will introduce you to a superb way of keeping that uppermost in your mind at all times.

Protect your dreams

We all need to dream a little and you should protect that right. Take time to dream and learn how to protect your precious dreams.

You can't afford the luxury of a single negative thought

Introduce this Shoeism into your life and into the lives of everyone you know. Be a wall of energy and simply don't allow negativity in. Given the power of the negative forces right now, you'll need this one to be the first Shoeism you adopt.

Give yourself permission to take time off. Alone

Ladies, stop the guilt. It's officially OK to be selfish sometimes and have time alone. Why do we forget this? Use this Shoeism as your justification for 'me time'.

Find your special place of tranquility

This is a lovely idea and you will enjoy spending the time making your own magical place of tranquility. It is a wonderful solitary activity and will stay with you for years as a failsafe source of calm and healing.

You can solve intractable problems while you sleep

Imagine if you could go to sleep and wake up with some of your problems gone. You can. Look at this Shoeism and introduce this wonderful technique into your problem-solving tool kit.

Live each day as if it were your last

Don't wait until something dreadful happens to realize how precious every day really is. See the strength you can get from repositioning yourself on this one.

Beware the psychic vampires

Who said vampires were dead? They are all around, and this tool will introduce you to the biggest destroyers of joy ever. Have a dip in – you too can become a vampire slayer.

Know where you get your energy

From this little gem you can learn what you need to do to renew your energy when it runs out. You can avoid wearing yourself out with the wrong behaviors. Useful for reading the energy levels of people around you, especially the people you live with.

Be a pane of glass

There is nothing like panic to bring on mindless aggression. All around us, anxiety and aggression are spilling into everyday encounters. Don't get sucked into others' outbursts and learn how being a pane of glass allows you escape.

Review each day positively

Be honest and see if you are too hard on yourself. Adopt this Shoeism and switch your perspective to a more nurturing view of your activities.

Don't own negative comments

Life is challenging enough without absorbing other people's negativity. I feel I can generate enough of my own – do you? If so, have a good look at this one.

You can never have too many shoes

Discover the magic of shoes in women's lives and realize that your obsession is shared by many.

Never live from a scarcity perspective

There is enough time and resources. Don't live your life from the viewpoint that there is not enough to go around.

Scarcity living means you try to control everything in order to ensure that there is enough. You also limit your opportunities. Let go...loosen up...embrace risk.

There are people who live their lives as if there is not enough of everything to go around. They feel life crowding in on them because they don't believe there is enough of them available for everyone in their lives.

They think that their family expects too much time and attention, and that their work is constantly making demands on their energy and intelligence. There is not enough money in their lives. Their bank account will never be full enough. It goes on and on.

❧ The scarcity life ❧

These people feel a great void inside them and worry that there is simply not enough! They are living what I call a 'scarcity life.' They view life from the perspective of 'not enough.'

They think that there is a famine out there, and so there is not enough to go around. Have you ever felt like this? Have a look around you and ask yourself this question. Am I living my life from a scarcity perspective?

People who live with this outlook can end up trying to control everything. They think that if they manage their time, they will control any wastage of time. They want maximum return, as they fear there is so little time. And in doing so, they send out a tight control message which puts off the prospect of any potential contacts.

I remember going to an international conference of speakers where I met a fellow speaker from my home city. I was much taken aback to be told that this lady could not waste time with me, as we were here to meet new people, not waste time with old ones.

I realised that she was trying to control everything; she felt there was a very limited time frame in which to meet all those people. She left me feeling bruised and certainly alienated. It made me wonder why she would not have thought that two of us could have networked far more effectively by pooling effort and resources.

ᦈ **What if?** ᦈ

Be open. Don't limit your opportunities. If you find yourself controlling everything and worrying that there is not enough, my advice is to loosen up and let go of this fear of scarcity. When you find yourself being short with people and trying to micro manage your interaction, just take a deep breath and loosen the controls.

Embrace risk. You can change your perspective if you really want to. Instead of asking what will happen, ask instead "what if?" What if I thought there was enough of everything? What if I trusted the universe to deliver the right people into my life? What if I took a deep breath and believed that there was enough of me, that I should trust myself? What if I believed that I am good enough to rise to any occasion?

What would the world be like then?

ᦈ **Look at yourself** ᦈ

Have a look at yourself and see if any of these elements are there, then question how you could turn them around. Try reframing the situation. If you feel a tightening sensation because you believe there is not enough, turn it around and ask yourself what if there was more than enough.

A good example is when someone asks you to spend an afternoon with them and you immediately say, "I haven't got the time." Imagine if you said to yourself, "I have all the time in the world. I will see what I can give to this person and I will trust that something will come of it."

Try abundance, it may change your life.

ༀ Scarcity thinking can ruin ༀ a business

Marian was a colleague of mine who definitely lived from a scarcity viewpoint. Her life was stalling. She was single and totally devoted to her business. It absorbed all her waking hours. She really believed that if she took her eye off the business, it would fail. She had no room for friends, family or anyone who was not a customer.

She was wound up like a spring from the effort of trying to protect her scarce resource, herself, from everyone. When the business was on the verge of failure, she finally turned to others for help and was truly astonished at the generous and unconditional help she received. Their abundance saved her. It was an eye opener for her. Her scarcity had almost broken her.

Conserve your inner essence

Think of yourself as a vessel with two openings. The top where liquid comes in and the bottom where it leaves.

If you keep emptying it, with work, family and friends and don't refill it with rest and calm, you will empty out. If you allow it to completely empty you will be in danger of getting sick.

Burn out occurs when you empty out all your resources.

I'll always remember the day someone said to me, "Veronica, you are so hard on yourself. You don't give yourself a break. You will empty out your life vessel." It was then that I discovered the metaphor of life being like a vessel full of liquid.

This life vessel has two openings, one at the top where liquid comes in – and one at the bottom where it drains out. You have to think of the liquid as your life essence, your energy, your spirit, and your joy of life. The challenge in your life is to keep the level of the liquid up near the top – and certainly never below the halfway mark.

❧ Are you doing too much? ❧

Look at your life and see how you are doing. Are you saying yes to everyone? Are you working too hard, either at home or in the workplace? Are you doing too much? Think about it, it's actually common sense that if you continuously empty the vessel, it will drain dry and you will become worn out.

Now look at how you are filling the vessel up. Have you actually stopped and thought about which activities fill up your essence? Do you know what activities renew you? If I asked you, could you immediately write down five things that are yours?

For example, what do you do to relax? Do you know what fills up your energy levels? The challenge is to be able to differentiate between the drainers and the renewers – and to keep track of them. You need to cut out the drainers and get more of the fillers.

Realistically, there are both wonderful and awful times in anyone's life. You know how wonderful you feel for the first few days after your annual vacation, before reality hits you again.

It is very good to take an annual vacation, as it lifts your spirits. One of the big differences between Europeans and Americans is the great love affair Europeans have with their vacations. In my native Ireland, the minimum is four weeks annual leave, in addition to nine public holidays.

The summer vacation is the highlight of the year, closely followed by the year end, with a complete close down of business at the end of December until early January. That is a major energy filler!

Have you looked at your fillers and drainers on a daily and weekly basis? I feel it is better to keep a close eye on the liquid on a daily basis, as it is not good to let all your energy drain away and to be so tired going on vacation that it is more a recuperative time than a recreational one.

✎ Keeping the vessel full ✎

Because life is life and unexpected things happen, I suggest that you have a threefold approach:

Take a look at the next 12 months, the next week and every day.

Look at the 12 months and mark in your vacation, your weekend breaks and public holidays like Thanksgiving. Make sure these times off are well-spaced throughout the year. It no good having a lovely first six months if you then never take a break from June until December, and you end up a wreck at the end of the year.

Now take a weekly view. Are you working every day? Where is your down time? Have you marked off time for energising activities? Have you marked off time to be with the people you love? Is there 'me' time in there?

Now take a daily view. Have you developed some good self-preserving habits? Do you take time each and every day to reflect, to listen to music, to breathe deeply, to look out the window? Make sure your five energisers get their place.

The last thing you must think about is that if you drain the vessel completely you will get sick. Your body will find a way to tell you. Look at the people in your life. How many of them have stress-related ailments? How many people do you personally know who have made themselves ill?

Don't let that happen to you.

My favorite daily fillers are:

- A short daily walk outside in the air
- A lovely hug
- A spot of reading
- Some of my favorite 'rubbish' TV programs like murder mysteries
- An energising chat with one of my favorite people.

My absolute drainers are:

- Dealing with negative people
- Lack of courtesy in people
- The untidiness of others
- Trying to energise switched-off people
- Lack of sleep

Now have a think. What are your fillers and drainers?
Have a look at this and quickly note your top five in each category.

Daily Fillers

1. _____
2. _____
3. _____
4. _____
5. _____

Daily Drainers

1. _____
2. _____
3. _____
4. _____
5. _____

Protect your dreams

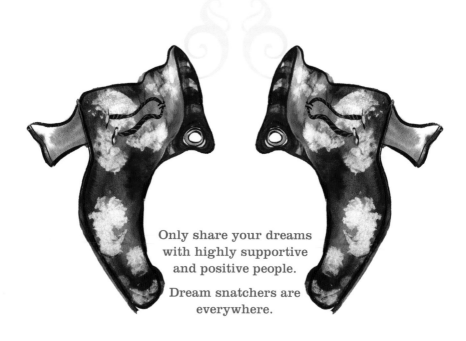

Only share your dreams
with highly supportive
and positive people.

Dream snatchers are
everywhere.

You would not expose your
naked baby to ice cold
conditions so don't expose
your fledgling dreams to ice
cold negative people.

Wait until your idea is better
developed and can withstand
constructive criticism.

✎ Don't share with the wrong people ✎

I always encourage people to have a huge, big purpose in their life and to dream big. Why not dream big, it's as easy as dreaming small? When you develop a fledgling dream, you get a glimpse of your new future. It could be a new business, a new job, a family or a new home. The main point is that it's your precious dream and you have just thought of it.

In the early stages of building a dream, you are very vulnerable. This is because you are unsure as to whether you are doing the right thing. You may be wondering if it is too big a dream and, equally importantly, if you will be able to deliver it.

Believe me, that is normal. I encourage all my people in the SHOES programs to have a really big dream. I have seen over the years the huge problems that arise when people share their dreams with the wrong people.

I always remember the first time I wanted to write a book and how I shared the thought with a colleague of mine. He looked at me with a skeptical eye and asked me what I knew about writing books. I buried that dream for another year before I resurrected the enterprise and acted upon it.

✎ Make your own notes ✎

<table>
<tr><td></td></tr>
<tr><td></td></tr>
<tr><td></td></tr>
<tr><td></td></tr>
<tr><td></td></tr>
</table>

❧ Rosemary's story ❧

I always remember Rosemary, who had joined up with a big franchise to sell health supplements. She was at the early stages when she came to work with me. She was very intelligent, a good saleswoman and she really knew her product.

Together, we worked out where she would like her business to be in five years time. This was her dream. She spent a good length of time developing it, and she was just getting her head into that successful space where it was becoming a viable proposition to her. Admittedly, it would take time and energy to accomplish, but her dream was now formulated and she was about to take her first steps.

She was out at dinner with her extended family and told her sister-in-law all about her dream. She laid it out, the targets, the marketing, the good, the bad and the ugly. Because it was so new to her, she also laid out her vulnerabilities and doubts. Can you guess what happened? Of course, the sister-in-law attacked and nearly killed the dream. It was like putting a naked baby out in the cold and throwing cold water on it.

Rosemary was devastated and came back to me saying that her dream was too ambitious. And what did she know about business anyway? It is extraordinary to watch how someone can absorb all the destructive negativity of others and allow their own dream to be subject to doubt – or even ended.

❧ Dream protection rules ❧

The dos

1. Firstly, always get comfortable with your dream.

2. Dream it, make friends with it, and become comfortable with it before you introduce it to strangers.

3. Do a vision board of your dream to make it tangible.

4. Set out the goals which will bring you to the dream.

5. Choose your confidantes carefully.

6. Only share your dream with open, positive, encouraging people.

The don'ts

1. Don't think others will readily understand your dreams.

2. Don't listen to everyone's advice.

3. Beware the power of envy.

4. Don't let others walk on your dreams.

5. Don't share until you are sure of yourself.

6. Never share your dream at the fledgling stage.

I would like you to enjoy one of Ireland's greatest poets, W.B. Yeats, on the subject of protecting dreams in his poem He Wishes for the Cloths of Heaven.

"But I, being poor, have only my dreams;
I have spread my dreams under your feet;
Tread carefully because you tread on my dreams."

Whatever else happens, always have dreams – but make sure you protect them.

You can't afford the luxury of a single negative thought

Challenge each and every negative thought.

Question it. Shake it. Look it up and down. Reframe it in positive terms. Look for the positive angle.

"I did not get that job" changes to "I now know the areas I need to work on to get the next job".

Don't let a negative thought settle in your mind.

Imagine not having any doubts! Imagine not constantly questioning yourself! Imagine being optimistic and believing that you will succeed at whatever you do!

Does that sound wonderful? Well, it's all yours if you remember one thing: you can't afford the luxury of a single negative thought.

❧ What is negative thinking? ❧

Negative thinking is a habit. Some people pass every idea or suggestion they encounter through a negative filter. They scan everything for danger, for problems, for their potential bad effect. They can't help themselves. Negative thinking is their default thought pattern.

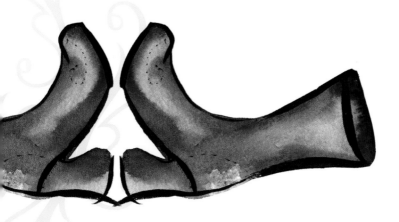

⤳ Do you think negatively? ⤳

Have a look at these questions to stimulate your questioning.

- ⤳ How do I react when I hear a new idea?
- ⤳ Do I see the problems before the possibilities?
- ⤳ Am I afraid of change?
- ⤳ Do I try to demolish ideas I don't like or that make me feel uncomfortable?
- ⤳ Do I exhaust myself looking around for danger?
- ⤳ Am I overly critical of myself?
- ⤳ Do I have problems accepting compliments or praise?

Do you automatically go to the negative side of things? If so, you need to let go of this. Have a good 'think' about your thinking!

∾ Effect of negative thinking ∾

Negative thinking has a corrosive effect on you and you become hard on yourself. You find yourself:

- Constantly finding fault with your actions
- Feeding your fears
- Limiting your potential
- Holding yourself back
- Never doing anything challenging for fear of failure
- Getting stuck in a rut

∾ Negative thinking has a deadening ∾ effect on those around you

- People become afraid to suggest new ideas to you.
- No one will ask you for advice because they know you will always see the problems.
- It kills spontaneity in others.
- It makes you a tricky person to live with.
- Work colleagues filter everything before they tell you.
- Honesty disappears because you are not seen as being open and fair in your assessments.

∾ How do I turn it around? ∾

The first thing is to be honest with yourself and see it for what it is. Don't excuse yourself and say that it is being realistic, pragmatic or conscientious. I constantly see negative thinkers use these words to wriggle off the hook. Take my advice – don't!

Practice analyzing your thoughts. Don't be a lazy thinker. Don't just think – go further and practice auditing your thoughts. Take every thought and examine it from all sides. See if it is negative. Be honest.

ꙮ Turn the negatives into positives ꙮ

Reframe every negative thought to see any positive elements. Take this thought as an example:

"I don't think the suggestion that we make a sales trip to Raleigh is good as I have already been there and there are no opportunities."

The reframing process involves establishing the facts and the inner motivations with questions like the following:

- ꙮ Is it a fact that there are no opportunities there?
- ꙮ Is it possible that I may be threatened by this suggestion?
- ꙮ Am I afraid I will somehow be found wanting?

You need to remove the fears and protective thoughts to allow the sentence to become more open and honest. Try this.

"On my last trip to Raleigh, I had limited success in getting buyers. That may be due to a number of factors. Let's look at them."

Then go a step further and actually reframe each sentence so that you view it in a positive way.

"I am open to taking a trip to Raleigh but I would like to plan it very well so that we can achieve our selling goals."

ꙮ Challenge every thought ꙮ

Move to a position of challenging every thought and of imagining what your life would be like if you cut out negative thinking. Go into every new initiative with the rigor of only thinking positively. You will be amazed at the difference it will make.

Everyone is scared at the start of something new, but if you ban negative thoughts then you build yourself a powerful ally. You turn every thought around and insist on a positive approach. As a process of banishing the terrible middle of the night fears it can't be beaten. Believe me I use it – all the time.

Give yourself permission to take time off. Alone

Being alone in a relaxing, enriching environment is a human right for women.

Give yourself permission to have time alone – with no tasks or responsibilities. Even a short time alone in silence is restorative.

Do you find it so hard to give yourself permission to do this? Plan your next time out now.

✌ Why do women not take time ✌ for themselves?

Being alone in a relaxing, enriching environment is a human right for women. It is essential to women's well-being to have time alone to think. Yet it is something few women manage to achieve.

When women become mothers, they sometimes change and believe that their family can't manage without them. They feel they need to be there to look after all the household management, and firmly believe that their households will fall apart without them.

I know this because I have seen it with my own eyes. No amount of talking gets these women to change. I recently ran a workshop for working women on visioning and planning. One of the women told me she had got up at 5am that morning to make dinner for her grown sons and husband so she could come to the workshop. When we brainstormed about changing their lives and she was pressed on one thing she would change, it was to stop cooking dinner one day a week.

Other women don't believe anyone can do the job, at home or in work, like they can.

They have a sort of 'superiority complex' that they are the best and no one else can be trusted. It is vital that they get over this. I have seen too many women end up sick or worse and, surprise surprise, their family gets over it and life goes on. Sadly, nobody is indispensable – except in their own mind!

Many women don't feel they deserve it. They are plagued by guilt. Women, in my view, are very prone to enduring the burden of guilt. I notice young women shaking off that yoke, but too many older women are held back by it.

In my childhood, we were told not to be 'forward' – to step back and not draw attention to ourselves. Does that sentiment ring a bell with you? If so, look into that and think about how you can get away from it.

❧ What are the benefits of spending ❧ time alone?

Solitude, even in brief snatches, can bring great benefits. It allows you time to think, to take a breather and to escape from your hectic life. It is hard to stay healthy if you are under constant pressure, with no release mechanism. The best creativity comes when you step outside your normal grind and just stop. Your brain gets to move away from the tiny details and concentrates on more abstract things.

I used to find it very difficult to get away and was always surrounded by people. In fact, I think that until a few years ago I dreaded being on my own. I began to realise what was happening when I came to understand, from Jungian psychology, that extrovert people are people who get their energy from others.

They enjoy going out and being with others. They are the kind of people, I feel, who have yet to discover the benefits of solitude. Jung's introverts are already on to this as they prefer time alone and get their energy from quietness and calmness.

I now try to get time alone every day and really crave it when I am unable to do so.

⤷ Make time for yourself ⤶

Try out these:

- ⤷ Go for a walk, no matter how short. Just go out the door and around the block or nearest park. I was in New York recently and I could not get over how peaceful Central Park was and how many people were sitting alone reading books.

- ⤷ Sit in a coffee shop and pause and breathe.

- ⤷ Resist picking up the phone to call someone. Go make coffee and sit and look at the garden.

- ⤷ Sit in your car for five minutes when you come home and gather yourself.

- ⤷ Go to work a little earlier and take a short walk or sit and relax for five minutes.

- ⤷ Go to bed a little earlier and relax. Don't turn on the telly. Just enjoy the solitude.

Look at your daily schedule and find your own time. I recommend that you become alive to the possibility of being alone.

Greta Garbo may well have had a point when she said, "I want to be alone."

Find your special place of tranquility

Establish a routine for when you need to become calm.

Find a favorite place – a special stretch of coastline or a quiet park. Go there and relax for 30 minutes. Do it frequently.

Your mind will associate that place with calmness. When you are stressed, the very act of being in that place will calm you.

Why do you need a place of tranquillity?

In this crazy, busy world where many of us are working ridiculous hours, it is especially important that you identify a special place of tranquillity for yourself. This is somewhere easily accessible that you can go to in times of stress or overload. You need this place because it provides an instant psychic healer for you. It works like this. You find a lovely place, like a stretch of park, a beach, a mountain walk, a section of a river bank, a boat in a river or bay or just somewhere you like to be.

You go there in times of calm and enjoy the place. You sit there and relax or go for a walk or a hike and soak up all the beauty and calmness of the place. Now here comes the magic. When you are feeling overcome or anxious, you go there and your system recognises the place and the feelings associated with it. The very fact of being there begins to calm and heal you.

ᕲ My place ᕘ

I have such a place. It is a stretch of coast near my home in Dublin and I have been walking there for years. As soon as I see the Irish Sea and the waves breaking on the seafront, I begin to feel well. I find the sea has that effect on me. I grew up only five minutes from the sea and we had seagulls sitting in our back yard whenever there were stormy conditions out on the waters of the sea.

They would come and hide out in our neighbourhood. I grew up walking our dog every day all along the seafront. I walked for miles to a bridge which led to an island called Bull Island. This was a bird sanctuary for migrating birds. Is it any wonder that I went on to graduate from college as a marine zoologist?

ᕲ Find your spiritual home ᕘ

Where does your love for nature surface? Go find out and make that your place of healing. Try to go there alone. Going there with a friend and chatting all the time is not the way to do it. It must be your place. You and your mind, body, spirit. Alone.

The secret is to find and cultivate the place right now. Do it when you least need it, so that it is in place for you when you do.

A wonderful bonus in life is to identify some place you can call your spiritual home. This can be a less accessible place, but somewhere you visit a couple of times a year and you know it will thoroughly restore you. My family live in Ireland, a place full of spiritual places, but by serendipity we have found the end of the beach in Naples, Florida, to be the place.

It is called Gordon's Pass and I know for certain that when I go there a few times a year, it will heal my spirit. My writing retreat is a world-famous spa in Ireland called Monart, where I wrote the majority of this book.

Have a think about this and see which places spring to mind as your everyday place of tranquillity and your spiritual home. As women, we feel reluctant to take this time for ourselves and to seek out our personal places. I suggest that you get over this and start the practice right now.

You can solve intractable problems while you sleep

Complex problems with many angles and no single obvious solution need a special approach. Rational, linear problem solving does not work.

You need the AHA approach. Explore all aspects of the problem and then let it incubate in your head. Sleep on it and let the unconscious mind take over. Often, you will think of the solution the next day.

Have you ever found some problems impossible to solve? Have you found that you can't unearth a solution because the best solution eludes you? You may need to look for a more creative way of thinking. You could benefit from practising AHA thinking.

When we solve problems, we first carry out a sequence of actions in our heads. To do this, we make a representation of the world in our minds – our understanding of what is happening at any given time. Our mental representation can influence the kind of thinking we engage in. In short, how you solve a problem depends on how you think of it, so it is vital to make the most accurate representation you can of any given situation.

It is useful to start your thinking about any problem by considering its very nature. In practice, I find that there are two major types of problems – reasonable and unreasonable problems. Before you begin any problem-solving exercise, you must decide which one you are looking at.

᫰ Reasonable problems ᫰

Reasonable problems are those to which the solution is clear, but you have to find a way to get from where you are now to that solution state. You find some means of reducing the difference between where you are in a problem and where you want to be. You visualise the end, find the now, and work out the steps to get you between the two. If you meet a blockage, you use sub-goals to get through the blockage. You keep moving forward all the time.

᫰ Linear thinking ᫰

Linear thinking works well for this kind of reasonable problem. This is because linear thinking allows you to progress through a series of logical steps, using inference to guide you from one step to the next. You make steady progress towards the solution.

᫰ Unreasonable problems ᫰

Unreasonable problems are those to which the solution is not obvious. In fact, the solution is nowhere to be seen. You often feel stuck, and can remain so until you have an AHA experience. This happens when the problem is represented in such a way that the solution becomes obvious. You suddenly accept that you do not know how to solve the problem. A new representation of the problem enables a new set of options.

The five stages of AHA thinking

To produce solutions to unreasonable problems, you must follow a process involving five separate and sequential steps. I call this the AHA THINKING PROCESS. Like any technique, the more you use it the better you become. Practice makes perfect.

1. Define the problem

First, you must clarify the purpose of solving this exact problem. You must work through misunderstandings and uncover all the layers of the problem. If you work through them, you will find the real problem.

It's crucial that you resist diving straight into solving a problem without spending time on defining its exact nature. Before you begin any problem-solving process, query all assumptions, determine any emotional dimensions, and ensure that you are solving the problem and not its symptoms.

2. Become absorbed

Start by immersing yourself in all aspects of the problem. This may seem obvious, but is often overlooked in pursuit of the instant solution. You must do a good job at this first stage of collecting raw materials or you will jeopardise all the other stages. So read all the paperwork, talk to the key people and visit the relevant sites. Take the necessary time, become an 'expert.'

3. Take it outside the box: use creative search techniques

You must learn and practice creative search techniques in order to bombard your mind and challenge all your comfortable and familiar thinking mechanisms. Your mind does not easily or readily go outside the box. It likes comfortable thinking patterns, so you must force it to be imaginative. Insightful thinking demands that you develop the ability to see deep within a problem to its underlying structure.

You need to go outside the parameters of the problem, even outside your own domain, to search for ways to stimulate your mind.

To see the problem from totally different viewpoints, you need the insight that often comes when you switch attention from one aspect of a problem to another.

Surprisingly, many novel ideas come from the new combination of old elements. So, techniques which force you to connect the different, opposing or strange are essential. Successfully seeing those combinations can depend on your ability to see relationships. Techniques which stimulate your mind to explore new paths or see new combinations are invaluable.

There are many such techniques but my favorite is one called 'rich text pictures,' in which you draw images rather than speak. It allows you to tap into your subconscious mind and escape the default thinking patterns with which we are all comfortable.

Other techniques like metaphors or analogies, when handled well, stimulate people to go way outside their usual thinking patterns and provide a space where genuinely new approaches are explored. Metaphors are a very powerful tool for liberating thinking.

You will find that random thoughts and novel ideas spark in your mind. Note them down. They are the beginnings of the ideas to come.

4.   Incubate the ideas

At this stage, make no direct effort. Leave the problem and all your new ideas alone. Let them incubate. It cannot be rushed or bypassed. Turn the problem over to the unconscious mind. There are different views on what actually happens. Some believe that, if we are stuck in a mental rut, then incubating allows that rut to disappear and we see things differently.

Another view is that we access our long-term memory, where we tap into a vast network of interlinked concepts and information. Whatever the reason, it is impossible to beat the success of 'sleeping on the problem.' Don't get tired with the process – persevere.

5.   Cognitive snap

After a period of incubation, the idea will appear to you out of nowhere. You make a breakthrough in your thinking. You'll say, "AHA, I know the answer." You'll experience the AHA effect. Believe me – if you have followed all the five stages, it **will** happen.

Live each day as if it were your last

Life is not a dress rehearsal; it's a one-off real show.

Why waste days, weeks, and months in futile activities.

Don't waste your life – live it. Live it hugely, gladly, fully.

Write your own eulogy. Decide what you want to be remembered for. Then live your life richly as you achieve it.

↬ Death changes everything ↫

I always live every day as if it were my last. In all reality, it very well could be.

In the last few years, a number of immediate family members and some close friends have died. I am sure this may have happened to you. I imagine it made you stop and think. The shock of losing so many key people in my life has made me stop and think about life and death in totally real terms. I now believe that until you really suffer grief at first hand, you can continue to discuss death in abstract terms.

Once you have felt its icy tentacles, it becomes a grim factor in your life and influences your outlook on life. It makes you see the preciousness of life, every minute of life. Your relationship with time changes totally. I used to see time as something that I didn't have enough of, but I realised that was the wrong attitude. There is the same amount of time for all of us; the challenge is how we use it. All good time managers tell you to grab time by the scruff of the neck and make it work for you. Otherwise, it drifts away.

When I was in my twenties, I thought that I had a lifetime in front of me and so I didn't panic about achievements. I set myself the goal of seeing a great deal of the world by the time I was forty. Luckily, the right career unfolded, which allowed me to reach that goal. Now, I see time as limited and frequently say that life is not a dress rehearsal, so stop practising for your real life. Get on with it; you might not be here tomorrow.

❧ Don't sleep on anger ❧

If you really subscribe to living each day as if it were your last then it makes perfect sense not to go to bed on your anger or with any row unresolved. It is a wonderful maxim to live by. You and your family know that you must make up before bedtime, as that is the rule.

This reframes people's attitude to anger and resentment. If you know that there is a time limit on your anger, and that you cannot bring your resentment into another day, then you have an inducement to move faster to see the other person's point of view. Try this out and make it your maxim to make peace before you go to sleep.

Don't take this message as sorrowful or depressing. Take it as being affirming and positive. I want you to wake up in the morning saying something like 'bring it on.' I am ready. This is the best day of my life. You can turn the intensity up or down to suit!

If you live every day as if it were your last, you will have one fun life.

❧ Make your own notes ❧

❧ The anniversary of my death ❧

I was struck ice cold by a poem by the American poet W.S. Merwin called The Anniversary of My Death. In it, he raises the possibility that in the past year I have passed over the very day that will turn out to be the anniversary of my death. He says:

**"Every year without knowing it I have passed the day
When the last fires will wave to me
And the silence will set out
Tireless traveler
Like the beam of a lightless star."**

He sees the end of life as the fires waving at him. If you think like this, you move your perception of death from being an abstraction to being a concrete reality. So having moved to that place, it seems easy to then think of living every day as if it were your last.

When you come to this place in your mind, it seems a good idea to try your best every day and to make it have a purpose.

Beware the psychic vampires

Listen carefully to people's comments. But don't accept them at face value – go behind to the intention.

Evaluate it. If it comes from a place of black negativity, you may be linked into a psychic vampire.

Psychic vampires seek to destroy enthusiasm and energy in others. Learn to recognize them.

Disengage, and don't let those comments into your head.

Psychic vampires are people who are full of negativity and they cannot see someone else happy or excited. They thrive on sucking the life out of your ideas or your vitality.

Why do we let others sabotage us?

It amazes me how we all let others sabotage us. We do this because we are not aware. We care too much about what others think of us and too little about what we think of ourselves. We give power to other people when we do this – we give away our energy and our power. Have you ever thought about how you feel when you have been with a really negative person? Don't you feel drained?

We should remove these people's influence from our lives, blank them out. They are sabotaging us at our core by extinguishing our inner light and energy. So why, if we know how we feel after being with these people, do we still let them zap us? This is a question that I ask myself all the time. When I have an idea for a topic that I want to write or speak about, I have learnt to guard it carefully. I only share it with a chosen few.

❧ How do you recognize ❧ a psychic vampire?

They are all around you, so here are some ways to allow you to quickly spot them.

Know their favorite phrases

- ❧ That's not a good idea – it will never work.
- ❧ Why would you do that?
- ❧ You have no qualifications for that.
- ❧ That is not possible.
- ❧ That has already been done and it never works.
- ❧ You look awful.
- ❧ Have you been ill?
- ❧ Oh dear, another of your projects.
- ❧ Why would you bother?

Know their behaviors

- ❧ You arrive full of excitement with great news, and you leave feeling depressed.
- ❧ You are in great form, and you leave feeling somehow in the wrong.
- ❧ You are happy and you feel you have been attacked, but it was done so subtly you cannot put your finger on what happened.
- ❧ You feel victimized in a group.
- ❧ You have a wonderful idea dashed just as you were explaining it.

❧ Psychic vampire scale ☙

Not all psychic vampires are the same: I see a scale of these negative people with three levels.

Level one

They drain the life out of you and your ideas. They do it by gently washing doubt and negativity over you. They have no energy. They can be energy sinkholes and you find all your energy seeping out of you into that hole. When you leave their company, you are somehow diminished.

Level two

These are people who go beyond energy draining and actively psyche you. They say and do things to bring you down. They may be doing it unconsciously. Sometimes, they are just projecting their own fears onto you. They see a challenging person, they feel fear, and you get smacked in the face with it.

Level three

These people are aware of what they are doing. They may be envious of your success or feel that you are shining too brightly. They know how to push your buttons. They know your hidden fears and vulnerabilities and target them with a few well-chosen words.

They are capable of inflicting psychic wounds that can take months or years to get out of your head. I am extremely wary of being around these people – or of letting them into my head in any way. Think of the Dementors in Harry Potter and the Order of the Phoenix. Dementors are wraithlike creatures in the Harry Potter novels who can suck the happiness and soul out of a person, making them feel like they will never be happy again.

✎ Handling psychic vampires ✎

- ✎ The first key is to realize they are there, that otherwise lovely people can have psychic vampire moments.

- ✎ Know the tell-tale signs, the phrases and the behaviors. Also, know how to recognize the symptoms of when you have been zapped.

- ✎ Know how to keep your own counsel, so be careful with whom you share your ideas and fears.

- ✎ Grow up and realize that certain people are bad for you and stay away from them. You may have to be courageous on this one.

- ✎ Understand that some people close to you can have these moments and let it be. Don't engage at those times.

✎ Limit their damage ✎

The number one action is to be vigilant and not internalize the negative comments. You recognize them as coming from a bad place, so don't let them into your mind. It is astonishing how we zero in on the most negative comment and give it high priority.

It is well known among presenters and trainers that, when they get the evaluation forms back, they flick through the 90 percent excellent marks and focus on the 10 or less percent who wrote some negative comments. It defies logic. I have seen trainers change a whole presentation because of one comment about the slides. They ignore the 25 comments saying it was a great class and focus on the one negative one.

Find your psychic vampires and run!

Know where you get your energy

Do you get your energy from quiet times alone or from mixing in company? It's usually one or the other.

Discover which option energises you the most when you are drained. Do you long for a bath with candles, or a night out with friends?

Choose your favorite then do it when you need to revive your energy.

"I am **so** tired" is a very common complaint from women today. Many women are tired – and some are actually exhausted. Do you hear yourself complaining about tiredness? How often do you say it out loud? If it is every day, then I think this Shoeism will help you greatly. It explores where different types of people get their energy. It is vital to know this, as it will help you understand yourself a little more.

⤳ Extraverts versus introverts ⤳

I came across the teachings of C. G. Jung on extraversion and introversion a few years ago and I think they help explain where we get our energy. He uses the concept of extraversion and introversion to explain the different ways in which people seek out and renew their energy. These words have a meaning in psychology that is different from the way they are used in everyday language.

Essentially, it looks at where you put your attention and get your energy. Do you like to spend time in the outer world of people and things (extraversion), or in your inner world of ideas and images (introversion)?

Extraverts like to be out in the world and they get their energy from ideas and interactions with people. They are the ones who, at the end of an exhausting week, will go out and party on Friday night. They may be tired, but they light up like a Christmas tree as soon as they meet their friends. The introverts would rather stick pins in their eyes than go partying at the end of an exhausting day. They head for the warm bath and the candles.

Everyone spends some time extraverting and some time introverting. Don't mix up introversion with shyness, as they are very different.

Which are you? Look at the descriptions on the following two pages and decide for yourself.

⤳ Knowing your type means you can ⤳ refill your energy in the right place

When you realise which you are, you can make plans to suit your needs. You either plan the gathering of friends when you know you need them, or firmly refuse invitations when you know you need to go home and be quiet.

❧ Introversion ❧

An introvert says things like:

- I like getting my energy from dealing with the memories, concepts, ideas, pictures, and reactions that are in my inner world, which is inside my head.
- My preference is for doing things alone or with one or two people with whom I am comfortable.
- Before I act, I take time to reflect so I have a clear idea of what I'll be doing when I need to take action.
- Sometimes I like the idea of something better than the actual reality.
- Ideas are quite tangible things for me.

They are often described as:

- Sometimes forgetting to check back with the outside world to see if the inner ideas actually match their experience
- Quiet and reserved
- Comfortable in their own company and liking to do activities on their own
- Liking to know just a small number of people well
- Too reflective and not reacting quickly enough

❧ Extraversion ☙

An extravert says things like:

- ❧ I often talk a problem out loud and understand it better when I hear myself explain it and listen to what others have to say.
- ❧ I like getting my energy from active involvement in events. I like having many different activities.
- ❧ I get energized by being out and about, and being around people.
- ❧ I like to energize other people.
- ❧ I like moving into action and making things happen.
- ❧ I usually feel comfortable and at home in the world.

They are often described as:

- ❧ Outgoing or a 'people person'
- ❧ Being comfortable in groups and liking to work with people
- ❧ Knowing lots of people and having a wide range of friends
- ❧ Not allowing adequate time to think options over so can sometimes jump too quickly into an activity
- ❧ Not stopping and planning the outcomes before starting a project

Be a pane of glass

You always have a choice about what you will do in a conflict situation.

If you are forced to listen to offensive and barbed comments, you become transparent like a pane of glass. You freeze, and let the destructive comments go right through you and on to infinity. You don't own them. They never touch you.

Being a pane of glass is a defence mechanism to protect you when you find yourself in a very uncomfortable situation, especially if you think you are being attacked verbally.

⊱ Today's aggression ⊰

It is amazing how aggressive people are these days. Stresses and high demands on people are producing more aggressive and angry people. I find that in work situations there is far more workplace bullying and conflict than ever before.

It seems to be a gradual process where there is less and less time – and less and less people – to do more and more. Expectations are going up in direct inverse proportion to the human resources available to deliver. Have you looked around a department store recently and thought, 'Are there any staff here at all?'

Do all the people you speak to on phone help lines have an edge of hostility in their voices? I believe we are finding ourselves in far more hostile situations than before and I think this Shoeism will be invaluable to you.

❧ What is the best thing to do? ❧

Imagine the comments coming at you. If you are a solid body mass, the comment hits you and is absorbed. It then has the potential to hurt and to make you react. A really good reaction to nasty negative comments is to change the image and become a transparent object – turn to glass.

The comment goes straight through you and out the other side and on to infinity. You do not retain any of it. It never touches you! As you get better at this and make it a part of your coping tools, you will be amazed at the effect it has on people. People who are nasty to put you off balance, see that it has no effect – and stop.

I have survived many encounters where there was an attempt to make things personal. I did my pane of glass routine and emerged very well. You will get the reputation of being self-contained and will be complimented on your professionalism.

When you combine this with the Shoeism 'Don't own negative comments,' you have a very powerful resource.

❧ Make your own notes ❧

❧ Provoking situations ❧

Have you been in these situations?

First of all, let's see if you can identify any situations that give you a clue to what I mean. Have you found yourself in any of these situations recently?

I have actually seen all of these in work environments.

❧ An episode where you felt you were on the receiving end of an unjustified attack

❧ You felt that someone was going for you and didn't know what to do

❧ You made a valid suggestion at a meeting but were undermined by a personal comment

❧ You realised someone was being personal and you had touched a raw nerve within them

❧ You found yourself reacting emotionally in a work situation at an inappropriate time

❧ You found yourself in a hostile situation because someone else was the bearer of bad news

❧ You were leading a team with volatile members who speak before they think

❧ You were with angry people who needed to vent their anger on someone

Do you have a situation in your mind? You are sitting there and something has happened and you feel threatened and unsure what to do.

✌ Our survival reactions ✌

Here are some really bad survival reactions you may have engaged in. Believe me, we have all had these reactions at one time or another.

- ✌ Snapped out a sarcastic reply
- ✌ Told them where to get off
- ✌ Burst into tears
- ✌ Sulked in silence for the rest of the meeting, building up a great big grudge
- ✌ Answered the personal remark with a more personal one
- ✌ Refused to answer but glared in a hostile fashion
- ✌ Got into a slanging match
- ✌ Allowed yourself to be sidetracked by a personal discussion
- ✌ Told them to put it where the sun doesn't shine
- ✌ Lost focus because you went inside yourself to process the remark

Review each day positively

Every night before you go to sleep, quietly review the activities of the day. Be kind.

Look hard for the positives. There is a positive in everything if you look hard enough. If you have difficulty finding it, switch your viewpoint.

When you have the positives, feed them into your brain so you go to sleep on a positive note

〜 Are you too hard on yourself? 〜

I honestly believe women are too hard on themselves; I too am guilty of this. I ask every woman I work with to tell me how they view themselves and they always expect too much and don't mind themselves enough.

This was brought home to me when I heard an interview with a woman politician who had just lost her seat after being an elected official for 10 years. She had an unusual take on it: she said that when men lost elections, they wondered what was wrong with the voters, and when women lost, they wondered what was wrong with themselves!

〜 Review the past 12 months 〜

I find it very powerful for women to sit down for 30 minutes, to go through the past 12 months and to note down the successes and disappointments across that time. Without fail, three things emerge:

- 〜 They can't remember what they have done in the past 12 months.
- 〜 The majority can quickly fill the page with disappointments but struggle to list the successes.
- 〜 They are surprised at their successes. They had forgotten them.

Women can pass onto the next thing too quickly and fail to notice how much they are actually doing – and so miss their successes. Successes must be celebrated, not used as launching pads for the next challenge. Every triumph, however small, should be thoroughly celebrated.

❧ Review each day ❧

The best place to start this new approach to celebrating all your successes is by reviewing each day from a positive angle. Each night as you go to sleep, take a look back at the day. Remember how you felt during the morning and pick out the successes throughout the day. For example:

- ❧ Did your meetings go well?
- ❧ Did you have a successful outcome to an interaction you were dreading?
- ❧ Did you finish something you had left undone for ages?
- ❧ Did you have a lovely time with your children?
- ❧ Did you spend time alone for the first time in ages?

Sometimes, you can underestimate the fact that having survived the day may be a success in itself. It might not seem like it, but the fact that you got through a difficult emotional day can be a triumph. You are okay and will get up tomorrow.

❧ Try reframing the negatives ❧

When you have difficulty seeing anything to celebrate in your day, you might need to take a closer look at everything and reframe it. Take each thing and look for the positive in it. If you can't see a positive, then I suggest that you lower your sights.

A smile from a stranger, a compliment or a small task done well can be looked at positively. Life can be a problem because of high dramas, but it can also be a problem because it is seen as boring. Don't let yourself live a life of quiet desperation.

ᴥ Major advantage of reviewing ᴥ each day positively

If you end your day on a positive note, you are sending a positive signal into your brain as you fall asleep. You know that your subconscious is still working away on your issues but in a positive way.

It's even better if you ask your brain to figure out the best way forward for some positive new idea you have. Ever notice that your nightmares involve bits and pieces of the things that happened in the day? Your brain is processing them all while you sleep. I am encouraging you to send your brain off on a positive note.

From this moment on, stop being hard on yourself and celebrate every success. Keep a bottle of something bubbly in the fridge...just in case.

ᴥ Make your own notes ᴥ

Don't own negative comments

If someone says something negative about
you – don't respond. Wait.
Respect the silence.

Let the comment hover in the middle of
the room – don't own it.

You will be amazed as you see the negative
comment return to the negative source...
"the negatoid".

They are perennially negative people
who cannot say anything positive,
even to save their life.

Life is hard enough without having to take on other
people's negative comments. If someone says some
negative things about you, don't respond. Wait. I
learnt this Shoeism the hard way.

Leave them where they belong

A number of years ago, I worked as a consultant reviewing the operations of organizations, and then helping them improve their performance. You ask a lot of questions and, not surprisingly, despite your best efforts, you can make people very nervous.

I remember one occasion when I met a team of twenty individuals and, although everything had been explained in advance and all the questions answered by the management, there was still a very hostile atmosphere in the room. Quite quickly, people started making negative comments about the management, about the process and eventually about the consultant, namely me. It was a very difficult situation orchestrated by a few individuals – but watched keenly by the majority.

I can't lie and say it didn't bother me. It did. However, I stayed very calm and, more importantly, very still. I let the comments hover in the air and I did not own them. I did not react and so they did not belong to me. So they moved back across the room to the people who uttered them.

The reaction of all the passive observers in the room was amazing. They saw that I was acting as if the words hadn't been spoken. When the comments were safely back with their owner, they were neutralised. This meant that I could proceed to open the meeting and to run the agenda as agreed.

It was amazing to watch how the wind went out of their sails and how they began to get involved in the normal way of running a meeting. I learnt that day that not owning negative comments can be the most powerful way of dealing with them. The best way not to be affected by negative comments is to be prepared for them and to know what you are going to do or not do.

Deflecting negative comments

Here are some principles for deflecting negative comments. I have learnt these over the years:

Own your own time and take your time

- There is no law that says you have to react.
- Listen until the end of the sentence.
- Don't interrupt.
- Breath more deeply the further they go.

Avoid the underlying emotion

- Don't react to the negative tone of the voice.
- Don't react to the emotion or quiver in the voice.
- Don't react to phrases such as "it's all very well for you but…"
- Let the anger wash over you.

Know the insulting phrases so you can duck them

- What would you know?
- You would never understand.
- Look at you…
- How would you know?

Remember my father's oft-used phrase, "sticks and stones may break my bones but words will never hurt me." That was a constant phrase in my childhood. Also remember that the most effective way of staying positive and centered is to let others keep their negative comments, even after they have shared them with you. Realise the power you have in you and understand the huge power of silence.

Make your own notes

| |
| |
| |
| |
| |
| |

You can never have too many shoes

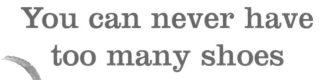

Face it – you can never have too many SHOES.

I don't care what anyone says, SHOES maketh the outfit – and the woman.

So indulge yourself and buy the best, the fanciest, the ultimate dream.

I really believe that you can never have too many shoes. Just consider for one moment all the variations a woman has to deal with on a daily basis. First of all there is the weather: wet, dry, snow or hot sun. And in Ireland, that can happen all in one day.

Then there are different styles of clothes: the flat casual, the trendy jeans, the business suit, the smart but comfortable travel outfit, the Saturday 'lunch with the girls' outfit, the cocktail dress, the ball gown – and that's just a few.

⤳ Why do we love shoes so much? ↝

I suspect our love affair with shoes is due partly to the fact that they are the one thing that stays the same size. So no matter how much you lose control of yourself and eat your own bodyweight in chocolate, your shoes still fit you. There is a lovely comfort in that, don't you think?

This love affair with shoes starts at a young age. Have you ever found yourself buying sparkly silver shoes for a one-year-old girl? My daughter and I did that last week.

We bought the most gorgeous little strappy silver shoes for a brand new cousin who was exactly three weeks old. We knew her mother would love them and keep them for her. With that sort of thinking, how could a girl grow up and not be programed to love shoes?

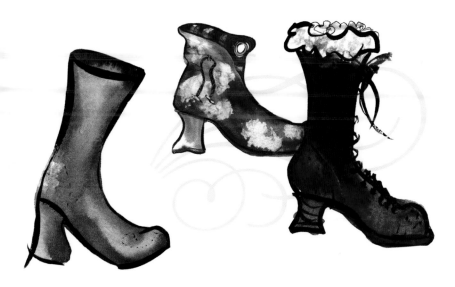

The love affair has taken on a new dimension in recent years. Designer shoes used to be something for the select few – movie stars, models and socialites – but not any more. Women of all ages and income lust after the ultimate designer shoe, often going without other things in order to buy them.

❧ Just how far would you go? ❧

There are only a small number of prestigious shoe designers and they have taken on the attributes of a prize, which has to be hunted down. This is really evident in the sales, where I have seen grown women (some of them my otherwise normal friends) turn into big game hunters, killing everything in sight to get to 'the' shoe.

No matter that it is the wrong size or the wrong color – it's a Jimmy Choo at half price. Sadly, I see the insanity of it and am still sucked in. Are you? I captured a pair of the red-soled Christian Louboutin (French shoe designer) shoes in the New Year sale in Saks last year, and really could not understand why my daughter made me give them back. They were only one size too small!

Why men don't get it

The issue of shoes really divides the sexes. For men, shoes are something you need to wear – nothing more. The only decision they have to make is whether to opt for black or brown, depending on their outfit.

For most women, however, they are an all-consuming obsession. I realized this when I launched the Shoes Program for inspiring women leaders. I gave a presentation to our local Chamber of Commerce and all the women present immediately got the concept and started asking questions about the Program and its content.

After I had finished, all the men wanted to know why it was called Shoes. When I began to explain how powerful a force shoes were in women's lives, I mentioned the allure of Manolo Blahnik. All the women nodded, but one guy piped up and asked me if Manolo Blahnik was a new business management strategy, like Six Sigma.

✎ Stand up in your stilettos ✎

I have seen high heels give a woman an air of authority. It's got something to do with the way your center of gravity changes and you have to alter your posture to stay upright when you walk. You can't slink along or slouch when you're wearing high heels – you are forced to stand up and take charge.

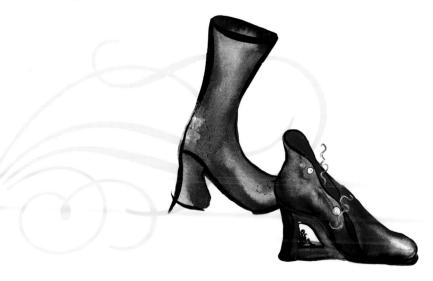

That is partly why I tell women in business who are making a presentation or pitching for business to put on the battle armor, but still remain feminine. Wearing gorgeous high heels lets you pull that off!

Stilettos have a particular place in women's lives. They are definitely a power tool. I was giving a talk to a group of women executives one time and suggested that they might like to embrace their femininity as they worked their way up the corporate ladder.

I suggested that they be like stilettos; gorgeously feminine but deadly at the same time. The women loved the concept so much that, when I set up my executive coaching program for women, I called it the Stiletto Program.

So go on ladies, go get your killer heels – in every color if need be!

⋙ Acknowledgements ⋘

I would like to acknowledge the inspiration, advice and encouragement of my friends, colleagues and family over the years. Their support has been invaluable to me.

This book has been a life time in germination and two years in writing and I would like to especially thank my friend Leanne Papaioannou without whose unfailing support I might have faltered along the way.

As in any project there are amazing people who contribute a huge amount to the overall project. Thank you to you all but in particular I would like to thank Trish Kelly for her beautiful design work and her endless patience with every change, Brendan Keane for his creative inputs at all stages, Laurence Jones for his excellent proofreading and my personal assistant Helen for all her incredible support.

This is a work where the shoes play a huge part and I am delighted to have Andrea Cleary's beautiful shoes drawings to illustrate each Shoeism. She loves shoes as much as I do.

All along the way I was buoyed up by the wonderful women with whom I worked and I found enormous pleasure in each and every Shoes program. I would like to give a huge thank you to all the participants in my programs who fired my imagination with their stories and their enthusiasm.

I would also like to thank all the people at Morgan James for their help with this project and particularly Rick Frishman for his wonderfully positive reaction to the idea and his excellent advice at the crucial initial stages.

Veronica Canning

ᨓ Author, speaker & consultant ᨓ

Veronica Canning has made her mark over the past three decades – both nationally and internationally – as one of the finest educational, inspirational and motivational communicators focusing primarily on the female audience.

She is an international consultant on strategic and creative thinking. Her clients include a number of Blue Chip organizations including Bristol Myers Squibb, Phillips and a number of Irish banks, as well as Irish government departments. Her client portfolio has extended with work for the European Union, in Bosnia Herzegovina. Veronica is a respected executive mentor and strategist with small to medium size companies and has provided consultancy services to national, regional development and enterprise organizations within Ireland.

Veronica has built the SHOES® BRAND around her innovative and progressive Mentor programs including:

- The highly acclaimed "SHOES® Programs for women", a revolutionary method of empowering the next generation of women business leaders focusing on entrepreneurs and small to medium businesses.

- The "STILETTO Program for female CEOs", focusing on developing their own personal strategies to drive both their business and empower themselves.

- The "RECESSIONISTAS Program" giving business women the tools that they need to drive their business through the recession successfully and emerge able to benefit from the upswing.

Through the SHOES PROGRAMS she has helped thousands of women to define their true goals and ambitions.

Previous Publications

As an **author** Veronica has published five books and a box of inspirational cards. She is frequently contacted for her opinions on various business practices embracing thinking for success. She is also a contributing writer to a number of magazines and newspapers.

She is also a much sought-after international speaker, with over 200 speeches under her belt, most recently in Syria as a keynote speaker at an International Women's Conference and for global companies and organizations launching women in business initiatives: including Deloitte, Double Click and Allied Irish Banks.

Veronica is also the **Immediate Past President** of the Professional Speakers Association of Ireland, the representative body for professional speakers in Ireland.

Please look up the companion box of thought provoking Shoeisms cards on www.shoeisms.com.

Contact her at www.veronicacanning.com

About the FREE Bonus

❧ Some questions for you ❧

Have you enjoyed using the SHOEISMS?

Do you want more of the SHOEISMS?

Would you like to get practical tools
in order to make them operational today?

❧ This is a huge opportunity for you ❧

Veronica Canning is offering all readers
the opportunity to get a weekly email communication
which focuses on a specific Shoeism.

Sign up to start to receive YOUR ezines on the SHOEISMS

Go to **www.shoeisms.com** and sign up now.

You will receive your ezine every week for a year and 4 weeks.

I'm sure that you will know lots of
women friends who are also trying to cope
with the challenges of being the perfect woman!

Be the one to introduce them to the magic of SHOEISMS.

Remember........tell a friend about the thought changing
power of Shoeisms.

Go on, be the sassy, successful woman you know you can
be every week!

BUY A SHARE OF THE FUTURE IN YOUR COMMUNITY

These certificates make great holiday, graduation and birthday gifts that can be personalized with the recipient's name. The cost of one S.H.A.R.E. or one square foot is $54.17. The personalized certificate is suitable for framing and will state the number of shares purchased and the amount of each share, as well as the recipient's name. The home that you participate in "building" will last for many years and will continue to grow in value.

Here is a sample SHARE certificate:

HABITAT FOR HUMANITY

THIS CERTIFIES THAT
YOUR NAME HERE
HAS INVESTED IN A HOME FOR A DESERVING FAMILY

1985-2005
TWENTY YEARS OF BUILDING FUTURES IN OUR
COMMUNITY ONE HOME AT A TIME

1200 SQUARE FOOT HOUSE @ $65,000 = $54.17 PER SQUARE FOOT
This certificate represents a tax deductible donation. It has no cash value.

YES, I WOULD LIKE TO HELP!

I support the work that Habitat for Humanity does and I want to be part of the excitement! As a donor, I will receive periodic updates on your construction activities but, more importantly, I know my gift will help a family in our community realize the dream of homeownership. **I would like to SHARE in your efforts against substandard housing in my community!** *(Please print below)*

PLEASE SEND ME _____ SHARES at $54.17 EACH = $ $_____

In Honor Of: _____

Occasion: (Circle One)   HOLIDAY   BIRTHDAY   ANNIVERSARY

     OTHER: _____

Address of Recipient: _____

Gift From: _____ *Donor Address:* _____

Donor Email: _____

I AM ENCLOSING A CHECK FOR $ $_____ PAYABLE TO HABITAT FOR HUMANITY <u>OR</u> PLEASE CHARGE MY VISA OR MASTERCARD *(CIRCLE ONE)*

Card Number _____ Expiration Date: _____

Name as it appears on Credit Card _____ Charge Amount $ _____

Signature _____

Billing Address _____

Telephone # Day _____ Eve _____

PLEASE NOTE: Your contribution is tax-deductible to the fullest extent allowed by law.
Habitat for Humanity • P.O. Box 1443 • Newport News, VA 23601 • 757-596-5553
www.HelpHabitatforHumanity.org